"Ben Mims hacks the high-powered heating and circ[...] frying machines so you can achieve pro-level crispy, [...] easy way, and upgrade your weeknight cooking. This book changes the game for foods like chicken wings and ribs, but offers surprises like creamy and caramelized eggplant, crispy okra, and an incredibly tender lemon cake that convinces me an air fryer isn't just a one-trick pony."

—**HUNTER LEWIS,** editor in chief at *Cooking Light* and *Food & Wine*

"Rethink the way you air fry, or cook in general, with this cookbook packed with delicious and healthy recipes from my favorite person, Ben Mims. From crispy classics, like Garlic-Rosemary Shoestring Fries or Fried Chicken Tenders, to surprising vegetables and desserts, like Mole-Braised Cauliflower or Strawberry Scone Shortcake, your mind will be blown with the diversity of meals you can make using this piece of equipment, while you save on an oily mess in your kitchen."

—**FARIDEH SADEGHIN,** culinary director at Munchies

"Ben Mims has a knack for understanding the way that real people cook today. His recipes bring out the flavor and complexity you seek in great food, with an understanding of the craziness in our busy day-to-day lives. You will be surprised and delighted by the amount of texture, enjoyment, and inspiration Ben has brought to the recipes in *Air Fry Every Day.* Not to mention, you won't believe all the fun and inventive things the air fryer can do."

—**CLAIRE KING,** head of culinary at Tasty

"In an oversaturated market of niche cookbooks and novelty cookware, Ben Mims manages to rise above, expanding the horizons of the air fryer thanks to his technical test-kitchen expertise and his creative culinary streak. I will follow Ben and his biscuits wherever he takes them! Despite my tiny Brooklyn kitchen, I'm compelled to make room for an air fryer, to buy his book, and to master his approach."

—**ALEXA WEIBEL,** senior food editor at *Rachael Ray Every Day*

AIR FRY EVERY DAY

CLARKSON POTTER/PUBLISHERS
New York

AIR FRY
EVERY DAY

75 Recipes to Fry, Roast, and

Bake Using Your Air Fryer

BEN MIMS

Photographs by Denny Culbert

Published in the United States by Clarkson
Potter/Publishers, an imprint of the Crown
Publishing Group, a division of Penguin Random
House LLC, New York.
crownpublishing.com
clarksonpotter.com

CLARKSON POTTER is a trademark and POTTER
with colophon is a registered trademark of Penguin
Random House LLC.

Library of Congress Cataloging-in-Publication Data
Names: Mims, Ben, author.
Title: Air fry every day : 75 recipes to fry,
roast, and bake using your air fryer / Ben Mims.
Description: First edition. | New York : Clarkson
Potter/Publishers, [2018] | Includes index.
Identifiers: LCCN 2018005804|
ISBN 9780525576099 (hard cover) |
ISBN 9780525576105 (ebook)
Subjects: LCSH: Hot air frying. | LCGFT: Cookbooks.
Classification: LCC TX689 .M57 2018 |
DDC 641.7—dc23 LC record available at
https://lccn.loc.gov/2018005804

ISBN 978-0-525-57609-9
Ebook ISBN 978-0-525-57610-5

Printed in China

Book and cover design by Ian Dingman
Photographs by Denny Culbert

10 9 8 7 6 5 4 3 2

First Edition

To J. and Otto & Sophie

CONTENTS

BREAKFAST AND BRUNCH

APPETIZERS AND SNACKS

MAIN EVENTS

VEGETABLES

SAVORY BREADS

SWEETS

INTRODUCTION

In this age of new, single-function gadgets, the air fryer may seem like it can only perform one role, but I've found that, like the newest tech update on the scene, it can do so much more and is more efficient than the "old ways." When I first mentioned the air fryer to friends and family, the most common response they gave me was "Repeat that again?"—the two words together didn't click in most people's brains. Yes, I know it sounds like one of the gadgets from the Island of Misfit Toys, but an air fryer actually does what its name implies, even if that name is a little nonsensical.

Most people reading this book now will already be air fryer groupies, first adopters who took this newest cooking machine and realized early on its potential to turn out convincingly healthier versions of deep-fried fare like chicken wings, french fries, and mozzarella sticks. For the rest of the readers, and perhaps even those early adopters looking to expand what they do with their air fryer beyond lightening up the deep-fried fare, I want to show you that the air fryer can certainly "fry" up those favorites, but it can also bake cakes, sear centerpiece meats, and roast some of your most favorite vegetables more quickly than a traditional oven. As an air fryer user, even I was surprised by some of the techniques I was able to pull off while developing recipes for this book. Crisping up cooked grains for salads—something I had never tried before because I didn't want to fuss with deep-frying grains—came out arguably

better than if they were cooked in oil. Tender yeast rolls baked up pillowy soft and I never had to heat up my kitchen with my large oven! And eggplant, cut into small wedges, cooked up silky smooth inside and caramelized outside, qualities I had only ever achieved in a deep-fryer but with a lot more oil than I was comfortable eating. But equally surprising? The crispness of french fries. The crackling skin of chicken wings. And doughnuts that had that delicate shattering exterior and fluffy interior I thought was only achievable from deep-fat frying. Whether you need no convincing or you need a book like this one to do the job for you, I promise you will be surprised and impressed by everything the air fryer can do.

Originally created almost a decade ago to give french fry–obsessed Europeans a way to make french fries in their tiny apartment kitchens without the hassle of heating gallons of hot oil and figuring out how to dispose of it afterward, today, large numbers of people in America, too, are cottoning on to the benefits of using an air fryer. It's about more than just cooking food with drastically less oil, which it does very well. The benefits of using an air fryer, as I see them, are many: Unless I'm cooking a large volume of food, it's a pain to turn on my large oven to cook for one or two people or reheat leftovers—the oven heats up my kitchen, turning it into an oppressive sauna, an unwelcome side effect even in the depths of winter. The air fryer cooks many foods that an oven can, but faster and better.

How? Well, air fryers use a heated coil (usually at the top) and a fan to circulate the heat around foods at convection oven rates. When foods cook in a regular oven, they create steam, but that hot, fast air in an air fryer efficiently whisks that excess moisture away. The result? Whole potatoes bake up crisper on the outside, pork ribs get exceptionally crisp crusts, and a whole cauliflower cooks perfectly tender inside at the same rate that its outer florets become lightly charred and crunchy. Those kinds of results are a godsend when you consider the fact that the food was not cooked using traditional, expensive, or stationary cooking equipment. Its portable size is a boon, too. I've talked to many enthusiasts who proclaim the joys of being able to have hot food easily, whether it's cooked in their RVs, boathouses, dorm rooms, or hotel rooms when they're on road trips, made in their kitchens during a home renovation when nothing in the kitchen actually works, or prepared on offshore oil rigs (!) where a singular catering-size kitchen isn't accessible to the crew.

Just as it can produce shatteringly crunchy meats and vegetables, it can bake up soft, tender cakes; beautifully coddled eggs; and thickened, unctuous rice porridge. Like any other appliance, mastering it is all about understanding its core capabilities and how to maximize them to achieve the desired outcome. I created the recipes in this book to take advantage of the air fryer's fast-heating ability, cooking only a few portions of food at a time, and making food where a crisp exterior or shorter cooking time actually improves the dish. Sometimes I use the air fryer like a traditional deep-fryer to get crispy shoestring fries (see page 55) and crackling-skin chicken wings

(see page 39) but without all the extra oil and calories and with better results. There's no risk of them turning soggy because they're not sitting in oil that's not at the proper temperature due to a drop or spike in heat, which is a constant headache when deep-frying with oil.

And at other times, I use it like a mini-convection oven, which is the most accurate description of its capabilities, to bake up fluffy lemon cake (see page 144); gooey, spoonable brownies (see page 151); and soft, tender yeast rolls (see page 130)—a boon when you want to whip up a sweet treat quickly or get another dish on the table without taking up more room in your oven.

That same convection quality makes the air fryer better at creating reduced sauces and glazes than on the stovetop or in a regular oven—easily and quickly transforming applesauce into apple butter, reducing marinades for meats and sauces for vegetables to sticky-finger licking perfection. It crisps up cooked grains (see pages 93–95, 122) wonderfully, breathing new life into your lunch meal prep; blisters shishito peppers (see page 51) like a restaurant's wok; and even cooks up fluffy, tender egg frittatas (see page 24) that make putting together this simple breakfast even easier.

Once you get your own air fryer, I think you'll fall in love with it, and I hope you'll use the recipes in this book as your guide to the many possibilities of these ingenious machines. No longer a funny-sounding novel appliance, I guarantee you'll find ways to incorporate it into your everyday cooking and make it just as essential as your home range.

AIR FRYER 101

How to Choose an Air Fryer Model

As with adding any new appliance to your arsenal of kitchen equipment, the most difficult decision is which one to buy. There are several models of air fryers on the market at the writing of this book, and I'm willing to bet that number will double by the time this book hits the shelves. Air fryers range from petite versions that take up about the same space as a small microwave to larger versions that can cook large amounts of food and are more like studio-size countertop ovens. Prices range from well under $100 to upward of $300. Some air fryer cooks swear by certain models, but for this book, I did lots of research to see which might be best for me. Ultimately, I decided to go with the fairly inexpensive 2.2-quart CRUX model to develop the recipes for this book because I wanted everyone who can afford an air fryer, no matter the price, to be able to use the recipes in this book with success. This means that the majority of the recipes are made to serve one or two people because of the machine's smaller cooking area. But rest assured, I also tested these recipes in large models and found the results just as good. In models with large fry baskets, feel free to, say, double the recipe for Spicy Dry-Rubbed Chicken Wings (page 39) to make enough for a large party. Or if you have the width, you can bake two Lemon–Poppy Seed Drizzle Cakes (page 144) side by side.

How to Use Presets

Every air fryer you might buy, like microwave ovens or multipurpose cookers, will come with preset cooking

---

CONVECTION OVEN-STYLE FRYERS

If you do purchase a combination convection oven/air fryer, like the Cuisinart Air Fryer Toaster Oven or the Breville Smart Oven Air, don't worry, you can still make all the recipes in this book in it, plus more since you won't be as limited to the size and shape of the tall, cylindrically shaped models. For most of the recipes, you won't have to change anything at all. To adapt any recipe in this book that utilizes the shape and height of the cylindrical models—like the Spicy Dry-Rubbed Chicken Wings (page 39) or Memphis-Style BBQ Pork Ribs (page 47), both of which are stood up on their ends and leaned against the wall of the air fryer basket—simply lay the food on its side in the extra space in the basket and cook as usual. For recipes like the Caesar Whole Cauliflower (page 104) or Cheesy Pull-Apart Garlic Bread (page 133), you may have to trim the top to fit or use a different-shaped loaf of bread that's shorter and wider.

temperatures and times for specific foods, set by their respective manufacturers. These presets are convenient for simple foods that fit the purpose, like reheating pizza or frying chicken. I experimented with these presets as guides at the beginning of my development, but ultimately tinkered with the temperatures and times to cook foods to a slightly higher quality without the "one size fits all" nature of presets. By all means, use those presets for the convenience, if you like, but once you see what the times and temperatures for each are, feel free to experiment yourself until you find the right combination for your favorite foods.

Shake, Stir, Flip

Though it's usually not necessary to adjust the foods while they're in the air fryer, thanks to the constantly circulating air, it's nevertheless a good practice to move some foods around to ensure they get the optimal amount of exposure to the hot air while cooking. For loose items like fries or okra, a simple shake will do. For smaller pieces of food like grains, it's helpful to stir them, lifting up any bits on the bottom of the basket or pan and moving them toward the top. And for wet foods like glazed tofu or soy-and-garlic chicken thighs, where the food is sitting in liquid that needs to reduce and glaze the meat or vegetable as it cooks, you'll want to flip them often so you don't end up with the bottom half completely wet and the top half unpleasantly dried out.

Don't Overload the Basket

Deep-fried foods that are free-floating in hot oil get heat transfer at every angle and on every available surface area. Since items cooked in an air fryer aren't suspended in oil, if you pack lots of fries into an air fryer, for example, the ones in the middle might not get as well cooked as those on the perimeter, which is getting the full force of the air fryer's powerful hot air. One way to remedy this is by shaking and turning foods a few times while frying to make sure

---

BASKET TIPS

Depending on how big the air fryer basket is in your particular model, some larger items, such as the Samosa Vegetable Pot Pie (page 137) or Cheesy Pull-Apart Garlic Bread (page 133), may take up most of the space in narrower baskets. If that's the case, line the basket with wide, crisscrossed strips of parchment paper or aluminum foil to create a sling that you can use to lift the foods out of the basket. Additionally, "air fryer liners," as they're sold on Amazon.com, are perforated rounds of parchment paper (used for bamboo steamers, as well) that are great for lining air fryer baskets, making cleanup just that much easier.

---

everything is evenly cooked. Another, more efficient way to combat this issue is to cook in smaller batches, so there's no worry about cold spots where the air is blocked.

Know Your Hot Spots

Think of your air fryer as if your oven and broiler were on at the same time. There's heat being circulated around the food constantly, cooking it from all sides, but that heat is primarily generated from above. For foods that are thin or small, like cutlets or shrimp, I don't flip because the heat circulates around them well enough and they're far enough from the heating element to avoid getting scorched. If you want to crisp up a particular side of the food, like the skin of a salmon fillet, it's good to position that side near the element so it gets extra heat exposure.

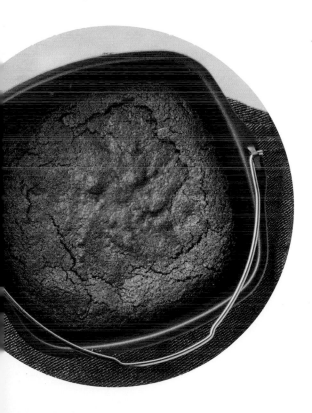

Use Pans to Expand Your Air Fryer Possibilities

Most foods you cook in your air fryer will be items like chicken wings or french fries—easy to retrieve with tongs or turn out onto plates. To expand the versatility of the air fryer—which is equally adept at creating glazes, baking cakes, and popping small grains—purchase a set of air fryer inserts, which are sold online or at cookware stores by many of the same manufacturers of the various air fryer models. Virtually all of them include a shallow "pizza" pan, a tall-sided "cake" pan, a silicone cooling mat, and metal racks to hold the pans. While not all these inserts are necessary to use your air fryer, it's a smart idea to get them (they range in price from $20 to $30) because they more than double the types of recipes you can make in your air fryer and really transform it into an all-in-one cooker.

Of all the inserts, though, the only one that I think is 100 percent necessary is the cake pan insert. To make baking achievable in the air fryer, you have to use a pan insert, and if I didn't include some baking in this book because of that, I would've felt I was doing you, the reader, a disservice. Not only important for baking, they make cleanup a breeze, too, especially when cooking sauced or sticky foods. However, I use the pan inserts only where necessary: Most of the recipes that need them are in the Breakfast and Brunch (page 21) and Sweets (page 143) chapters. The pans come in both round and square shapes to fit your particular air fryer, but the shape doesn't affect the cooking times in the book, as we tested baking recipes

TO PREHEAT OR NOT TO PREHEAT

I've found that most air fryers do not require preheating before using—therefore, I do not call for preheating in these recipes (great time savings). If your model does require it, simply preheat it before you start prepping each recipe, as you would your regular oven, so that it's good to go when you're ready to air fry. Along these same lines, some models require you to reset the time and temperature every time you remove the basket to check on your food, so be prepared for that. Or better yet, ask questions when buying your air fryer and avoid those models with that handicap. Similarly, a couple of models don't allow you to set the temperature above 390°F, while others go up to 410°F. The models I used for testing all allowed me to go to 400°F, which is the highest temperature I call for in this book. If your particular model doesn't heat above 390°F, you can still make the recipes in this book that call for cooking at 400°F, but they may require 2 to 5 minutes more in cooking time to match perfectly with the doneness and visual cues I have indicated in those recipes.

in both shapes. Aside from keeping cake batters in their place in the air fryer, they're also great for containing sauces, glazes, and marinades for meat; small grains like quinoa and rice that would otherwise fall through the basket holes; and other foods that might need a little extra support underneath. If you don't want to buy a set of inserts or the cake pan insert, you can just as easily use a 6- or 7-inch metal cake pan, available at any baking cookware store, or disposable round aluminum foil pans, which are very cheap and are sold in most grocery stores or online via Walmart .com or Webstaurantstore.com as "takeout" containers.

All the pan inserts have a metal handle on top to make lowering and lifting them out of the air fryer basket easy. But if you're using a cake pan or foil pan, use two pairs of tongs as pinchers to grab opposite sides of the pan and lift it out. What's great about the inserts, in particular, is that they can be cooked in and then transported right to the dinner table for serving.

How to Use Oil in the Recipes

Even though air fryers can cook up food without added oil—in fact, many people who buy them do so expressly for their ability to use no oil whatsover—the appearance of most air-fried foods is improved greatly with just a little added oil, but no more than you'd normally put on vegetables or meat to roast or sauté them. One tablespoon of oil tossed with vegetables softens their skins and enhances their char. The same goes for meats, where a little oil helps to imbue their

exteriors with an appealing caramelized color. For typically deep-fried foods with a breadcrumb coating like fried chicken or fish sticks, it's easier to coat them in oil by using cooking spray. There are many organic and natural cooking spray options on the market now, so I feel comfortable recommending them, especially once you see the benefits of using them on fried foods to get that perfectly golden brown hue. Choose brands that use olive oil or coconut oil, or purchase an oil sprayer, such as a Misto, which allows you to use your own favorite oil. Just be careful to spray the foods before you add them to the air fryer, not once inside the basket, since many manufacturers warn that cooking sprays can damage the interior nonstick coating of the air fryers themselves (similar to nonstick skillets).

And thanks to that nonstick surface, cleaning your air fryer is a breeze. Whether still warm or completely cooled, the inside of the air fryer can usually be wiped clean of any spills or splatters with just a damp paper towel. For the basket, some warm water and a soapy sponge, like you would use to clean any dish, suffice perfectly.

DRIED HERBS AND SPICES

Because air-fried foods are cooked using superheated air and they cook relatively quickly, I use a lot of dried herbs and spices. Doing this accomplishes two goals: It helps prevent the herbs from burning, which is a risk when using fresh herbs if there's not enough liquid present to keep them moist. And it also packs the foods with more concentrated flavor, something that would typically be built up over longer cooking times.

GET TO KNOW YOUR AIR FRYER

I see you've brought your new air fryer home, unpacked it, and taken off all the stickers and plastic. And you're ready to get cooking . . . like, this exact instant. No worries. I got you covered!

I obviously want you to make all the recipes in this book to see how versatile the air fryer is, but right now, I want you to get familiar with your new machine and all its functions, and see how it can cook ordinary, everyday foods that you most likely already have in your kitchen.

Frozen Foods

Though I cover the gamut of recipes that work well in your air fryer, if you have a bag of frozen french fries, chicken tenders, or any frozen food that calls for being fried or baked, this is the easiest place to start. As a general rule, simply reduce the temperature on the package by 25°F and reduce the cooking time by 25 percent to cook in the air fryer. For example, if a package calls for you to cook frozen veggie burgers at 425°F for 25 minutes, cook them in the air fryer at 400°F for 18 to 20 minutes, making sure to start checking the food on the lower end of the time range. Once you get a feel for how strong your air fryer is, you'll be able to tinker with the times and temperatures to get them just right.

Toast

If toasting 1 slice of bread, lean it against the wall of the air fryer basket. If using 2 to 4 slices, lean them against each other, like forming the shape of a tent, to fit more slices in the basket. Set the air fryer to 400°F and toast to your desired doneness. I've found that the number of minutes needed to make toast in the air fryer is comparable to those on the dials of a toaster (as in, if you toast your bread on a "3" in your toaster oven, it will take about 3 minutes to toast your bread). The timing will, of course, depend on the type, thickness, and freshness of your bread.

Bacon and Sausage

While we're making toast for breakfast, let's talk about eggs. I've found that there's not really a good way to make plain eggs in the air fryer (they're best mixed with other ingredients like in the frittatas and baked eggs in the Breakfast and Brunch chapter, starting on page 21); I tried making scrambled eggs and even after 30 minutes, the results weren't pretty or even slightly cooked. But while you're scrambling or frying your eggs on the stove, you can thankfully get the rest of breakfast cooked in the air fryer, especially typically messy or greasy bacon slices and sausage patties. For either, lay as many slices or patties as will fit in the basket in a single layer and cook at 400°F to your desired doneness, between 4 and 8 minutes (cooking from frozen doesn't affect the cooking time here). And if you bought one of those handy and useful air fryer insert sets (see page 13), you can use the included wire racks to elevate your bacon or sausage off the bottom of the basket to ensure more even heating around them.

Cookies

While I didn't develop air fryer–specific cookie recipes for this book (because the inherent nature of cookies doesn't translate well to the machine), the appliance is perfect for those times when all you want is to break off a square of prepared cookie dough and bake yourself a cookie. Just like with the aforementioned frozen foods, bake the cookies at 25°F less and for 25 percent less time than the package directs, then adjust from there until you find the right cooking time for your favorite brand of slice-and-bake or break-and-bake cookies. For the break-and-bake type of cookies, such as those made by Nestlé Toll House, where the package directs you to bake the cookies at 350°F for 12 to 15 minutes, I experimented a few times until I found that air frying the cookies at 320°F for 10 minutes was just perfect. If you have frozen balls of cookie dough from your own recipe, those will work in an air fryer, too. Just use the same time and temperature math and adjust until you've got a winning algorithm for that precious cookie.

Leftovers

A surprising food to try out in the air fryer is that slice of cold, leftover pizza in your refrigerator (don't lie to me, I know it's there). Instead of acting like you really love cold pizza (no one does) or heating it in the microwave until it's rubbery and sad, place it in the air fryer basket and cook at 400°F until it's revived, the cheese is re-melted, and the crust is crisp on the bottom again (!!!). It will take between 4 and 8 minutes, depending on the thickness and shape of the pizza. The air fryer is also perfect for reviving leftover fried foods from restaurants or your delivery orders—no more soft, soggy french fries, egg rolls, and wings reheated in the microwave. As you may have noticed, I generally recommend 400°F as the ideal temperature for the air fryer to get started because it's similar to roasting in your oven at 425°F, but faster and with crispier results. When in doubt with any new food, start at that temperature and check on the food as many times as you need until whatever you're cooking is as heated through and as golden brown as you like.

Meal Prep

As I found while developing most of the recipes in the Vegetables chapter (page 97), the air fryer is ideal for cooking vegetables for your weekly lunch meal prep kits. Cubes of sweet potato, halved Brussels sprouts, and chopped eggplant cook up perfectly in the air fryer. If you season them simply with olive oil, salt, and pepper, the vegetables can be divided up and used in grain bowls and salads or however you like, easily adaptable in playing well with a range of cooked grains, greens, and sauces. To help you get started, I created a simple chart of all the vegetables you can make in the air fryer (see page 99). More than any other use, I think these vegetables will be the most relevatory and make you the most excited to get air frying!

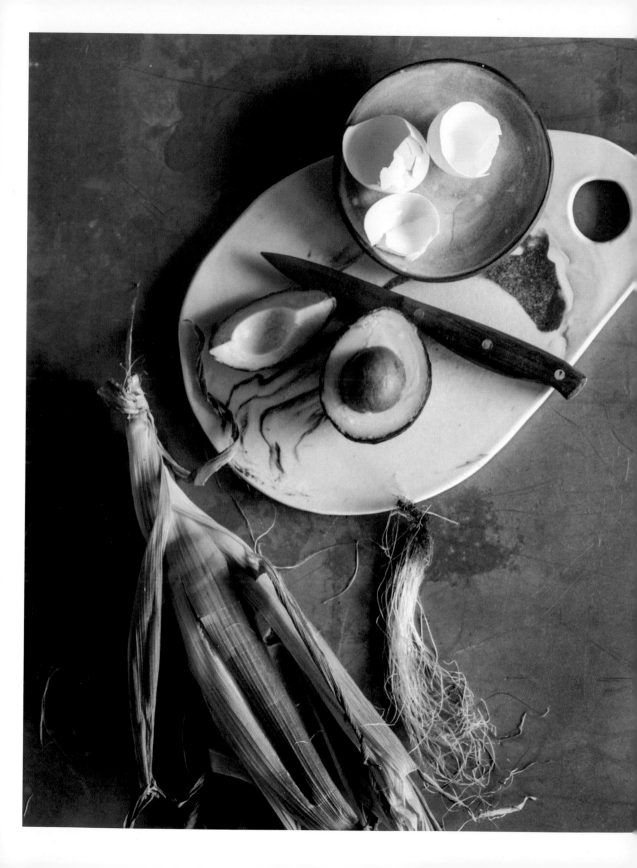

BREAKFAST AND BRUNCH

BAKED EGGS WITH KALE-ALMOND PESTO AND OLIVES

1 cup roughly chopped **kale leaves,** stems and center ribs removed

¼ cup **olive oil**

¼ cup grated **pecorino cheese**

3 tablespoons **whole almonds**

1 **garlic clove,** peeled

Kosher salt and **freshly ground black pepper**

4 large **eggs**

2 tablespoons **heavy cream**

3 tablespoons chopped pitted mixed **olives**

Toast, for serving

Switch It Up:

If you don't want to make the kale pesto for these eggs, simply substitute ¾ cup of your favorite homemade or store-bought pesto in its place and cook as stated in the recipe.

Baked eggs are a luxury because they take more time and effort than a quick scramble or fried egg. But here, they're just as quick to throw together and bake up with enough time to get the orange juice and coffee on the table and maybe even sit through a morning news segment. Feel free to use any store-bought or homemade pesto you have on hand for these eggs, but if you have the time, make this kale pesto to add an extra dose of greens to your morning.

SERVES 2

1. In a small blender, puree the kale, olive oil, pecorino, almonds, garlic, and salt and pepper to taste until smooth.

2. Crack the eggs into a 7-inch round cake pan insert, metal cake pan, or foil pan, then spoon the kale pesto over the egg whites only, leaving the yolks exposed. Drizzle the cream over the yolks and swirl into the pesto.

3. Cook at 300°F until the eggs are just set and browned on top, 10 to 12 minutes. Sprinkle the olives over the eggs and serve hot with toast.

BUTTERNUT SQUASH AND RICOTTA FRITTATA

1 cup cubed (½-inch) **butternut squash** (5½ ounces)

2 tablespoons **olive oil**

Kosher salt and **freshly ground black pepper**

4 fresh **sage leaves**, thinly sliced

6 large **eggs**, lightly beaten

½ cup **ricotta cheese**

Cayenne pepper

Switch It Up:

Not a butternut squash fan? Feel free to use another cubed squash or sweet potatoes in its place. And if you happen to already have leftover cooked pieces of squash or sweet potato in your fridge, you can use them here. Scatter them over the sage as directed but only cook for 4 minutes to warm through before continuing with the recipe as written.

Squash and sage is a classic autumnal combination, and I eat them together in virtually every meal as soon as the weather starts to turn chilly. This is one of my favorite uses for it: a tender frittata dotted with large dollops of ricotta cheese and dusted with cayenne. In the air fryer, the process is even more efficient since you're able to roast the squash until tender and then pour in the eggs and cook the frittata, all in just over 30 minutes.

SERVES 2 OR 3

1. In a bowl, toss the squash with the olive oil and season with salt and black pepper until evenly coated. Sprinkle the sage on the bottom of a 7-inch round cake pan insert, metal cake pan, or foil pan and place the squash on top. Place the pan in the air fryer and cook at 400°F for 10 minutes. Stir to incorporate the sage, then cook until the squash is tender and lightly caramelized at the edges, about 3 minutes more.

2. Pour the eggs over the squash, dollop the ricotta all over, and sprinkle with cayenne. Cook at 300°F until the eggs are set and the frittata is golden brown on top, about 20 minutes. Remove the pan from the air fryer and cut the frittata into wedges to serve.

CHIMICHANGA BREAKFAST BURRITO

Breakfast burritos are a staple of my weekend morning routine, and there's not much that can improve upon them. Except this chimichanga. Because there's no oil to make the tortilla greasy, it air fries up super crispy, like a burrito wrapped in a giant tortilla chip. You can customize the filling to your taste, so feel free to add cooked sausage, bacon, or ham to make these meat-friendly, or leftover roasted vegetables for a healthier option. And if you're really feeling up to it, make several burritos, wrap them in plastic, and freeze for up to 1 week so you can have a crispy, hot breakfast chimichanga whenever the craving hits. (To reheat the chimichanga from frozen, cook at 350°F for 15 minutes—no need to thaw.)

SERVES 2

2 large (10- to 12-inch) **flour tortillas**

½ cup canned **refried beans** (pinto or black work equally well)

4 large **eggs**, cooked scrambled

4 **corn tortilla chips**, crushed

½ cup grated **pepper jack cheese**

12 **pickled jalapeño slices**

1 tablespoon **vegetable oil**

Guacamole, **salsa**, and **sour cream**, for serving (optional)

1. Place the tortillas on a work surface and divide the refried beans between them, spreading them in a rough rectangle in the center of the tortillas. Top the beans with the scrambled eggs, crushed chips, pepper jack, and jalapeños. Fold one side over the fillings, then fold in each short side and roll up the rest of the way like a burrito.

2. Brush the outside of the burritos with the oil, then transfer to the air fryer, seam-side down. Cook at 350°F until the tortillas are browned and crisp and the filling is warm throughout, about 10 minutes.

3. Transfer the chimichangas to plates and serve warm with guacamole, salsa, and sour cream, if you like.

TOMATO AND CORN FRITTATA
WITH AVOCADO DRESSING

At the apex of summer, my kitchen is filled with cherry tomatoes. I eat them like candy and cook them in just about every meal. I adapted my favorite summer frittata using these tomatoes for the air fryer, and it works even better because I never have to heat up my oven. The tomatoes are first salted to remove excess moisture and concentrate their flavor, then baked up in the frittata and served with a creamy avocado-and-basil dressing to enhance the summer vibes.

SERVES 2 OR 3

1. Place the tomatoes in a colander and sprinkle liberally with salt. Let stand for 10 minutes to drain off their excess moisture. Transfer the tomatoes to a bowl and stir in the corn, milk, dill, and eggs. Season with salt and pepper and whisk to combine.

2. Pour the egg mixture into a 7-inch round cake pan insert, metal cake pan, or foil pan and place the pan in the air fryer. Cook at 300°F for 15 minutes, then sprinkle with the Monterey Jack and cook at 315°F until the cheese has melted and the eggs are set, 5 minutes more.

3. While the frittata cooks, in a medium bowl, mash the avocado with the lime juice until smooth, then stir in the olive oil, basil, and scallion.

4. Remove the pan from the air fryer, cut the frittata into wedges, and serve with some of the avocado dressing.

½ cup **cherry tomatoes**, halved

Kosher salt

½ cup fresh or thawed frozen **corn kernels**

¼ cup **milk**

1 tablespoon finely chopped fresh **dill**

6 large **eggs**, lightly beaten

Freshly ground black pepper

½ cup grated **Monterey Jack cheese**

1 **avocado**, pitted and peeled

2 tablespoons fresh **lime juice**

¼ cup **olive oil**

8 fresh **basil leaves**, finely chopped

1 **scallion**, finely chopped

Note:

If you have extra time or can plan ahead, use kernels from the air-fried corn in the Elote Corn and Cilantro Salad (page 115) instead of the fresh or frozen ones called for here.

BUTTERMILK BISCUITS

2½ cups **all-purpose flour**

1 tablespoon **baking powder**

1 teaspoon **sugar**

1 teaspoon **kosher salt**

½ teaspoon **baking soda**

8 tablespoons (1 stick) **unsalted butter**, chilled and cut into small cubes

1 cup **buttermilk**, chilled

As a born and bred Southerner, I eat a lot of biscuits. I often make a large batch of them once a month, and stash most of them in the freezer for whenever the craving hits. But with the air fryer, I can make a small batch and have fresh, dinner roll-size biscuits in less than 30 minutes that taste like they're from a traditional oven.

MAKES 16 BISCUITS

1. In a large bowl, whisk together the flour, baking powder, sugar, salt, and baking soda. Add the butter and use your fingers to break apart the butter pieces while working them into the flour mixture, until pea-size pieces form. Pour the buttermilk over the flour mixture and, using a rubber spatula, mix together until the ingredients are just combined.

2. Turn the dough out onto a well-floured surface and pat it into a disk, ½ inch thick. Using a 2-inch round cutter, cut out 16 biscuits. Place half the biscuits in a single layer (their edges should just touch) in the air fryer and cook at 325°F until the biscuits are golden brown and fluffy, about 18 minutes. Serve the biscuits hot. Cook the remaining biscuits or freeze for up to 1 month.

COCONUT BROWN RICE PORRIDGE
WITH DATES AND CARDAMOM

1 cup canned **coconut milk**

½ cup cooked **brown rice**

¼ cup **unsweetened shredded coconut**

¼ cup packed **dark brown sugar**

½ teaspoon **kosher salt**

¼ teaspoon **ground cardamom**

4 large **Medjool dates**, pitted and roughly chopped

Heavy cream, for serving (optional)

Making fried rice is a great way to use leftover rice, but I also love to use it to make rice porridges, such as this breakfast pudding, which feels like dessert but is a little healthier. I use brown rice for extra nuttiness and air fry it in coconut milk with dried coconut and cardamom, and sweeten it with brown sugar and dates. The air fryer reduces the porridge just enough to thicken it and caramelizes the top to perfection. Swap out the brown rice for other cooked grains, different sweeteners for the brown sugar, or other dried fruits for the dates to make your ultimate breakfast porridge.

SERVES 1 OR 2

1. In a 7-inch round cake pan insert, metal cake pan, or foil pan, stir together the coconut milk, rice, shredded coconut, brown sugar, salt, cardamom, and dates and place in the air fryer. Cook at 375°F until reduced and thickened and browned on top, about 23 minutes, stirring halfway through.

2. Remove the pan from the air fryer and divide the porridge among bowls. Drizzle the porridge with cream, if you like, and serve hot.

CHOCOLATE–WHITE CHOCOLATE BANANA BREAD

In an air fryer, baking up banana bread is much quicker, thanks to the convection-like heat and less actual batter to bake. Not your traditional banana bread, this version has cocoa powder in the batter and includes walnuts for crunch and white chocolate for creamy sweetness. It's perfect for your daily breakfast, or warmed up and served with ice cream for a great weeknight dessert.

SERVES 4

6 tablespoons plus 2 teaspoons **all-purpose flour**

¼ cup **Dutch-process cocoa powder**

½ teaspoon **kosher salt**

¼ teaspoon **baking soda**

1½ ripe **bananas**

½ cup **sugar**

¼ cup **vegetable oil**

3 tablespoons **buttermilk** or **plain yogurt** (not Greek)

½ teaspoon **vanilla extract**

1 large **egg**

6 tablespoons chopped **walnuts**

6 tablespoons chopped **white chocolate**

1. In a medium bowl, whisk together 6 tablespoons of the flour, the cocoa powder, salt, and baking soda. In another medium bowl, mash the bananas until very smooth. Add the sugar, oil, buttermilk, vanilla, and egg and whisk until smooth. Pour the wet ingredients over the dry ingredients and whisk until just combined.

2. In a third bowl, toss the walnuts and white chocolate with the remaining 2 teaspoons flour until evenly coated. Add the nuts and chocolate to the batter and stir until incorporated. Scrape the batter into a 7-inch round cake pan insert, metal cake pan, or foil pan and smooth the top. Transfer the pan to the air fryer and cook at 310°F until a toothpick inserted into the middle of the bread comes out clean, about 30 minutes.

3. Remove the pan from the air fryer and transfer to a wire rack to cool for 10 minutes. Unmold the banana bread from the pan and let cool completely on the rack before slicing into wedges to serve.

APPLE CIDER DOUGHNUT HOLES

Remember the days when from-scratch doughnuts were too much of a hassle to make at home? Yeah, those days were right before you read this recipe. Because of the air fryer, you can absolutely have easy, quick, fresh mini doughnuts in no time at all (as in, in less than 20 minutes). These doughnuts are light and airy, thanks to the buttermilk and apple cider, and their simple applesauce icing really brings the fall flavor home.

MAKES 10 MINI DOUGHNUTS

1. To make the doughnut holes: In a bowl, whisk together the flour, granulated sugar, baking powder, baking soda, salt, and nutmeg until smooth. Add the buttermilk, cider, and egg and stir with a small rubber spatula or spoon until the dough just comes together.

2. Using a 1-ounce ice cream scoop or 2 tablespoons, scoop and drop 10 balls of dough into the air fryer basket, spaced evenly apart, and brush the tops lightly with oil. Cook at 350°F until the doughnut holes are golden brown and fluffy, about 6 minutes. Transfer the doughnut holes to a wire rack to cool completely.

3. To make the glaze: In a small bowl, stir together the powdered sugar, applesauce, vanilla, and salt until smooth.

4. Dip the tops of the doughnuts holes in the glaze, then let stand until the glaze sets before serving. If you're impatient and want warm doughnuts, have the glaze ready to go while the doughnuts cook, then use the glaze as a dipping sauce for the warm doughnuts, fresh out of the air fryer.

For the doughnut holes:

1½ cups **all-purpose flour**

2 tablespoons **granulated sugar**

2 teaspoons **baking powder**

1 teaspoon **baking soda**

½ teaspoon **kosher salt**

Pinch of **freshly grated nutmeg**

¼ cup plus 2 tablespoons **buttermilk**, chilled

2 tablespoons **apple cider** (hard or nonalcoholic), chilled

1 large **egg**, lightly beaten

Vegetable oil, for brushing

For the glaze:

½ cup **powdered sugar**

2 tablespoons **unsweetened applesauce**

¼ teaspoon **vanilla extract**

Pinch of **kosher salt**

GIANT BUTTER-PECAN ROLL
WITH CINNAMON-CREAM GLAZE

8 ounces store-bought **pizza dough**

All-purpose flour, for dusting

2 tablespoons **unsalted butter**, melted

¼ cup packed **dark brown sugar**

¼ cup chopped **pecans**

¼ teaspoon **kosher salt**

1 tablespoon **Lyle's Golden Syrup**, maple syrup, or dark agave syrup

½ cup **powdered sugar**

1 ounce **cream cheese**, at room temperature

1 tablespoon **milk**

⅛ teaspoon **ground cinnamon**

There's nothing more satisfying than a cake-size version of arguably one of the best breakfast treats of all time: cinnamon rolls. Fortunately, that format works great with the air fryer—the giant roll bakes up fluffy and golden. Though still topped with a decadent cinnamon-cream cheese icing as tradition, I switched up the flavors here to reflect my favorite ice cream flavor: butter pecan. This stellar treat serves two sensible people who are eating it with maybe some eggs or bacon on the side, but I won't judge if you decide to keep the whole thing for yourself—I can't deny that I haven't already.

SERVES 2

1. Using a rolling pin, roll the pizza dough out on a lightly floured work surface into a rough 12 x 8-inch rectangle. Brush the dough all over with the melted butter, then sprinkle evenly with the brown sugar, pecans, and salt, then drizzle with the syrup. Using a pizza cutter or knife, cut the rectangle lengthwise into 8 equal strips. Roll up one strip like a snail shell, then continue rolling each spiral up in the next strip until you have one giant spiral.

2. Cut a piece of parchment paper or foil to the size of the bottom of your air fryer basket and line the bottom with it. Carefully lay the spiral in the air fryer and cover with a round of foil cut to fit the size of the spiral. Cook at 325°F for 15 minutes. Remove the foil round from the top and cook the roll until golden brown and cooked through in the middle, about 10 minutes more.

3. Meanwhile, in a bowl, whisk together the powdered sugar, cream cheese, milk, and cinnamon until smooth.

4. Once the roll is cooked, let it cool in the basket for 10 minutes, then carefully lift it out of the air fryer using the parchment paper bottom as an aid. Transfer the roll to a plate and pour the icing over the roll to cover it completely. Let the roll and icing cool together for at least 10 more minutes to set before cutting into wedges to serve.

APPETIZERS
AND SNACKS

SPICY DRY-RUBBED CHICKEN WINGS

In the absence of oil to crisp up the chicken wings' skins, which is the best part of eating them, a new technique was devised by J. Kenji López-Alt, the author of *The Food Lab* and a wizard in food science, to get crispy chicken wings in the oven. He proposed rubbing baking powder onto raw chicken wings. Once soaked into the skins and heated in the oven, the powder expands and bursts the chicken skin cells, making the wings super crispy. Don't worry about all the science of how it works, though—just know it *does* work. And the result is even better in the fryer, thanks to the force of the air, which expands the fat in the chicken skins even more, making these wings virtually indistinguishable from the deep-fried versions . . . except for the lack of super-greasy fingers after eating them. These "dry-style" air-fried wings are also relatively healthier, swapping out the traditional Buffalo-style bath of butter and hot sauce for the slow-burn of cayenne coating and a simple brushing of melted butter at the end. If you're a classic-Buffalo fiend, I've got you covered with a variation, too.

SERVES 2 TO 4

1. Place the chicken wings on a large plate, then sprinkle evenly with the baking powder, cayenne, and garlic powder. Toss the wings with your hands, making sure the baking powder and seasonings fully coat them,

(recipe continues)

1¼ pounds **chicken wings,** separated into flats (wingettes) and drumettes

1 teaspoon **baking powder**

1 teaspoon **cayenne pepper**

¼ teaspoon **garlic powder**

Kosher salt and **freshly ground black pepper**

1 tablespoon **unsalted butter,** melted

Blue cheese dressing and **celery and carrot sticks,** for serving

Classic Buffalo Wings

If you prefer saucy traditional Buffalo chicken wings, simply omit the cayenne from the recipe, and when the wings are cooked, toss in a bowl with ½ cup mild hot sauce, such as Frank's, and 4 tablespoons melted unsalted butter until well coated. Serve hot.

Go Basic:

Wanna make some plain wings to have as is or with your own favorite sauce? Simply omit the cayenne, garlic powder, and butter, and cook as directed, still using the baking powder method so that the chicken wings get super crispy.

until evenly incorporated. Let the wings stand in the refrigerator for 1 hour or up to overnight.

2. Season the wings with salt and black pepper, then transfer to the air fryer, standing them up on end against the air fryer basket wall and each other. Cook at 400°F until the wings are cooked through and crisp and golden brown, about 20 minutes. Transfer the wings to a bowl and toss with the butter while they're hot.

3. Arrange the wings on a platter and serve warm with blue cheese dressing and celery and carrot sticks.

LEMON-PEPPER CHICKEN DRUMSTICKS

Drumsticks are my favorite part of the chicken: rich and moist from the dark meat and perfect for handheld eating. Growing up, my grandmother would shower store-bought lemon-pepper seasoning on fried chicken, and it hit all the salty, savory flavor notes perfectly. For this updated version, I take a cue from the air-frying technique for my Spicy Dry-Rubbed Chicken Wings (page 39) and rub the drumsticks with baking powder along with pepper and garlic powder. Once air fried and crispy, I shower them with fresh lemon zest, adding brightness to cut through the crunchy skin and rich meat.

SERVES 2

2 teaspoons **freshly ground coarse black pepper**

1 teaspoon **baking powder**

½ teaspoon **garlic powder**

4 **chicken drumsticks** (4 ounces each)

Kosher salt

1 **lemon**

1. In a small bowl, stir together the pepper, baking powder, and garlic powder. Place the drumsticks on a plate and sprinkle evenly with the baking powder mixture, turning the drumsticks so they're well coated. Let the drumsticks stand in the refrigerator for at least 1 hour or up to overnight.

2. Sprinkle the drumsticks with salt, then transfer them to the air fryer, standing them bone-end up and leaning against the wall of the air fryer basket. Cook at 375°F until cooked through and crisp on the outside, about 30 minutes.

3. Transfer the drumsticks to a serving platter and finely grate the zest of the lemon over them while they're hot. Cut the lemon into wedges and serve with the warm drumsticks.

TRIPLE-COCONUT SHRIMP

½ pound peeled and deveined medium **shrimp** (tails intact)

1 cup canned **coconut milk**

Finely grated **zest of 1 lime**

Kosher salt

½ cup **panko breadcrumbs**

½ cup **unsweetened shredded coconut**

Freshly ground black pepper

Cooking spray

1 small or ½ medium **cucumber**, halved and seeded

1 cup **coconut yogurt** (or dairy yogurt)

1 **serrano chile**, seeded and minced

Go Basic:

To make plain fried shrimp, omit the coconut milk, lime zest, and shredded coconut. Set up a breading station with 1 cup all-purpose flour, 4 large eggs, lightly beaten, and 1 cup panko breadcrumbs in separate shallow bowls, and season each with salt and pepper. Working one at a time, coat each shrimp in the flour, dip in the egg, and dredge in the breadcrumbs. Transfer the shrimp to a wire rack set over a baking sheet and continue with the recipe.

There's no denying the appeal of coconut shrimp—crunchy, sweet, and easy to eat, like a meaty popcorn kernel. But they can be a mess to fry up, which makes them a perfect candidate for the air fryer. These shrimp are marinated in coconut milk, then coated in breadcrumbs and more coconut before getting cooked up to crispy perfection and served with a cooling-yet-spicy coconut yogurt. That's three hits of coconut and none of the excess grease; I can't think of a better sales pitch than that.

SERVES 2 TO 4

1. In a bowl, combine the shrimp, coconut milk, lime zest, and ½ teaspoon kosher salt. Let the shrimp stand for 10 minutes.

2. Meanwhile, in a separate bowl, stir together the breadcrumbs and shredded coconut and season with salt and pepper.

3. A few at a time, add the shrimp to the breadcrumb mixture and toss to coat completely. Transfer the shrimp to a wire rack set over a baking sheet. Spray the shrimp all over with cooking spray.

4. Transfer the shrimp to the air fryer and cook at 400°F until golden brown and cooked through, about 4 minutes. Move the shrimp to a serving platter and season with more salt.

5. Grate the cucumber into a small bowl. Stir in the coconut yogurt and chile and season with salt and pepper. Serve alongside the shrimp while they're warm.

HERB AND LEMON BREADCRUMB–STUFFED BLOOMING ONION

1 large **yellow onion** (14 ounces)

1 tablespoon **olive oil**

Kosher salt and **freshly ground black pepper**

¼ cup plus 2 tablespoons **panko breadcrumbs**

¼ cup grated **parmesan cheese**

3 tablespoons **mayonnaise**

1 tablespoon fresh **lemon juice**

1 tablespoon chopped fresh **flat-leaf parsley**

2 teaspoons **whole-grain Dijon mustard**

1 **garlic clove**, minced

I love stuffed artichokes, but, like most people, I hate preparing them. And a deep-fried blooming onion is super craveable and fun to share, but too labor-intensive to fry up. This recipe cuts out the work of both dishes and creates a flavorful hybrid that works great as a vegetarian main or as a side dish for the Chile-Rubbed Rib Eye (page 79).

SERVES 2

1. Place the onion on a cutting board and trim the top off and peel off the outer skin. Turn the onion upside down and use a paring knife, cut vertical slits halfway through the onion at ½-inch intervals around the onion, keeping the root intact. When you turn the onion right side up, it should open up like the petals of a flower. Drizzle the cut sides of the onion with the olive oil and season with salt and pepper. Place petal-side up in the air fryer and cook at 350°F for 10 minutes.

2. Meanwhile, in a bowl, stir together the panko, parmesan, mayonnaise, lemon juice, parsley, mustard, and garlic until incorporated into a smooth paste.

3. Remove the onion from the fryer and stuff the paste all over and in between the onion "petals." Return the onion to the air fryer and cook at 375°F until the onion is tender in the center and the breadcrumb mixture is golden brown, about 5 minutes. Remove the onion from the air fryer, transfer to a plate, and serve hot.

CHILE-BRINED FRIED CALAMARI

Fried calamari is my go-to bar snack, but unfortunately, if not executed well, it easily soaks up excess oil and becomes soggy and greasy. In the air fryer, there's no worrying about that, so you're guaranteed crispy, nearly greaseless calamari. I like to "quick brine" the calamari in pickled pepper juice to infuse it with more flavor and "fry" up some peppers alongside it to add interest to the pile of fried squid. A rosemary-infused garlic mayo is the perfect foil for this spicy, crunchy appetizer.

SERVES 2

1 jar (8 ounces) **sweet or hot pickled cherry peppers**

½ pound **calamari bodies** and **tentacles**, bodies cut into ½-inch-wide rings

1 **lemon**

2 cups **all-purpose flour**

Kosher salt and **freshly ground black pepper**

3 large **eggs**, lightly beaten

Cooking spray

½ cup **mayonnaise**

1 teaspoon finely chopped **rosemary**

1 **garlic clove**, minced

1. Drain the pickled pepper brine into a large bowl and tear the peppers into bite-size strips. Add the pepper strips and calamari to the brine and let stand in the refrigerator for 20 minutes or up to 2 hours.

2. Grate the lemon zest into a large bowl then whisk in the flour and season with salt and pepper. Dip the calamari and pepper strips in the egg, then toss them in the flour mixture until fully coated. Spray the calamari and peppers liberally with cooking spray, then transfer half to the air fryer. Cook at 400°F, shaking the basket halfway into cooking, until the calamari is cooked through and golden brown, about 8 minutes. Transfer to a plate and repeat with the remaining pieces.

3. In a small bowl, whisk together the mayonnaise, rosemary, and garlic. Squeeze half the zested lemon to get 1 tablespoon of juice and stir it into the sauce. Season with salt and pepper. Cut the remaining zested lemon half into 4 small wedges and serve alongside the calamari, peppers, and sauce.

MEMPHIS-STYLE BBQ PORK RIBS

Growing up near Memphis, I became loyal to their signature "dry" ribs early on in life, preferring them to the "wet," or sauced, kind found elsewhere. There are many theories about how best to cook ribs (boil first then grill, or barbecue slow and low the whole way?), but in the air fryer, you can have tender, pull-apart ribs in a fraction of the traditional time. The spice rub ensures a crunchy, caramelized exterior "shell" as well, so there's nothing missing here except the hefty barbecue grill and all the mess that comes along with it.

SERVES 2

1 tablespoon **kosher salt**

1 tablespoon **dark brown sugar**

1 tablespoon **sweet paprika**

1 teaspoon **garlic powder**

1 teaspoon **onion powder**

1 teaspoon **poultry seasoning**

½ teaspoon **mustard powder**

½ teaspoon **freshly ground black pepper**

2¼ pounds individually cut **St. Louis–style pork spareribs**

1. In a large bowl, whisk together the salt, brown sugar, paprika, garlic powder, onion powder, poultry seasoning, mustard powder, and pepper. Add the ribs and toss and rub the seasonings into them with your hands until they're fully coated.

2. Arrange the ribs in the air fryer basket standing up on their ends and leaned up against the wall of the basket and each other. Cook at 350°F until the ribs are tender inside and golden brown and crisp on the outside, about 35 minutes. Transfer the ribs to plates and serve hot.

MASALA-SPICED ONION RINGS
WITH MINT-MAYO DIPPING SAUCE

1 large **red onion**
(14 to 16 ounces)

¼ cup **garam masala**

2 tablespoons **sweet paprika**

2 tablespoons **curry powder**

2 tablespoons **kosher salt**, plus more as needed

2 cups **all-purpose flour**

6 large **eggs**, lightly beaten

2 cups **panko breadcrumbs**

½ cup **mayonnaise**

2 tablespoons finely chopped fresh **mint**

2 teaspoons fresh **lemon juice**

1 **scallion**, finely chopped

Cooking spray

Ketchup, for serving

Onions pair particularly well with Indian spices, so when I developed these onion rings, I wanted to flavor them with spices used in Indian cuisine to add zest and fun to the typical, rote onion ring. Instead of calling for dozens of different spices, use garam masala and curry powder spice mixes to get the job done, with a little extra paprika and salt for color and flavor.

SERVES 2 TO 4

1. Trim the ends from the onion and peel away the papery outer skin. Cut the onion crosswise into ¾- to 1-inch-thick slices, then separate the slices into rings, discarding the feathery skin between the rings.

2. In a small bowl, whisk together the garam masala, paprika, curry powder, and salt. Place the flour, eggs, and breadcrumbs in three separate shallow bowls and season each with one-third (2 tablespoons plus 2½ teaspoons) of the spice mixture. Dip 1 onion ring in the spiced egg, dredge in the flour, then repeat with the egg and flour once more. Dip the ring back into the egg again, then coat in the spiced breadcrumbs. Repeat to coat all the onion rings and arrange them on a wire rack set over a baking sheet. Place the onion rings in the freezer and chill until firm, at least 30 minutes or up to 1 week.

3. Meanwhile, whisk together the mayonnaise, mint, lemon juice, and scallion in a bowl and season with salt. Refrigerate to marry the flavors in the sauce while the onion rings freeze.

4. When ready to fry, spray 5 or 6 of the onion rings liberally with cooking spray and arrange them loosely in the air fryer basket, laying some flat and leaning some against the side of the basket. Cook at 375°F until the onion rings are tender and the breading is golden brown and crisp, about 10 minutes. Season with more salt once they come out of the fryer and continue frying as many onion rings as you like. Serve hot with the mint-mayo sauce and ketchup on the side.

Go Basic:

To make plain onion rings, simply omit all the spices. Season the flour, egg, and breadcrumbs with salt and freshly ground black pepper. And if you only have large yellow or white onions, you can substitute them just as easily for the red onion.

SHISHITO PEPPERS WITH GREEN GODDESS

Shishito peppers stir-fried in a wok are great, but I would put these air-fried versions up against the traditional ones any time. The peppers still blister and pop like in a wok, but with much less oil, making this recipe healthier and less messy. To offset the charred (and sometimes super spicy!) flavor of the shishito peppers, I love serving them with this creamy, cool Green Goddess-style dressing, which is just as good for dipping virtually any roasted vegetable.

SERVES 2 TO 4

6 ounces **shishito peppers**

1 tablespoon **vegetable oil**

Kosher salt and **freshly ground black pepper**

½ cup **mayonnaise**

2 tablespoons finely chopped fresh **basil leaves**

2 tablespoons finely chopped fresh **flat-leaf parsley**

1 tablespoon finely chopped fresh **tarragon**

1 tablespoon finely chopped fresh **chives**

Finely grated **zest of ½ lemon**

1 tablespoon fresh **lemon juice**

Flaky sea salt, for serving

1. In a bowl, toss together the shishitos and oil to evenly coat and season with kosher salt and black pepper. Transfer to the air fryer and cook at 400°F, shaking the basket halfway through, until the shishitos are blistered and lightly charred, about 6 minutes.

2. Meanwhile, in a small bowl, whisk together the mayonnaise, basil, parsley, tarragon, chives, lemon zest, and lemon juice.

3. Pile the peppers on a plate, sprinkle with flaky sea salt, and serve hot with the dressing.

SPICED SPF (SWEET POTATO FRIES) WITH GARLIC SOUR CREAM DIP

2 tablespoons **olive oil**

1½ teaspoons **smoked paprika**

1½ teaspoons **kosher salt**, plus more as needed

1 teaspoon **chili powder**

½ teaspoon **ground cumin**

½ teaspoon **ground turmeric**

½ teaspoon **mustard powder**

¼ teaspoon **cayenne pepper**

2 medium **sweet potatoes** (about 10 ounces each), cut into wedges ½ inch thick and 3 inches long

Freshly ground black pepper

⅔ cup **sour cream**

1 **garlic clove**, grated on a Microplane grater

Sweet potato fries (SPF) often get a bad rap because they don't fry up as crisp as regular potatoes. But these air fryer SPFs cook up with remarkably crunchy exteriors and are coated with lots of spices to balance the often too-sweet spud.

SERVES 2

1. In a large bowl, combine the olive oil, paprika, salt, chili powder, cumin, turmeric, mustard powder, and cayenne. Add the sweet potatoes, season with black pepper, and toss to evenly coat.

2. Transfer the sweet potatoes to the air fryer (save the bowl with the leftover oil and spices) and cook at 400°F, shaking the basket halfway through, until golden brown and crisp, about 15 minutes. Return the potato wedges to the reserved bowl and toss again while they are hot out the fryer.

3. Meanwhile, in a small bowl, stir together the sour cream and garlic. Season with salt and black pepper and transfer to a serving dish.

4. Serve the potato wedges hot with the garlic sour cream.

GARLIC-ROSEMARY SHOESTRING FRIES

The air fryer was made for fries, so it's no surprise that it does a great job cooking a potato to crisp perfection. To capitalize on that effect, I made these shoestring fries, which "fry" up super crunchy and golden. Eat them out of hand by the palmful or use them in place of store-bought potato sticks. At your next party, triple this recipe and cook in batches, then pile the fries high on a giant plate and set them out for a crowd-pleasing party snack that is more impressive than a bowl of nuts.

SERVES 2

1. Place the julienned potatoes in a large colander and rinse under cold running water until the water runs clear. Spread the potatoes out on a double-thick layer of paper towels and pat completely dry.

2. In a large bowl, combine the potatoes, oil, and rosemary. Season with kosher salt and pepper and toss to coat evenly. Place the potatoes in the air fryer and cook at 400°F, shaking the basket every 5 minutes and adding the garlic in the last 5 minutes of cooking, until the fries are golden brown and crisp, about 18 minutes. Transfer the fries to a plate and sprinkle with flaky sea salt while they're hot.

1 large **russet potato** (about 12 ounces), scrubbed clean and julienned (like matchsticks)

1 tablespoon **vegetable oil**

Leaves from 1 sprig fresh **rosemary**

Kosher salt and **freshly ground black pepper**

1 **garlic clove**, thinly sliced

Flaky sea salt, for serving

Classic French Fries

My aim was to develop the most creative potato recipes I could for this book, but I couldn't leave out your basic, classic french fry, for which the air fryer was originally invented. These fries are markedly better than a regular oven-baked fry, since the convection crisps the outside without drying out the inside.

To make them: Cut 1 large russet potato into ½-inch-square sticks. Rinse with water and toss with oil just as instructed in the shoestring fry recipe, then fry at 375°F for 25 minutes, until browned and crispy, shaking the basket every 5 to 7 minutes to make sure they're browning evenly.

SPIRALIZED POTATO NEST
WITH SPICY TOMATO KETCHUP

1 large **russet potato** (about 12 ounces)

2 tablespoons **vegetable oil**

1 tablespoon **hot smoked paprika**

½ teaspoon **garlic powder**

Kosher salt and **freshly ground black pepper**

½ cup canned **crushed tomatoes**

2 tablespoons **apple cider vinegar**

1 tablespoon **dark brown sugar**

1 tablespoon **Worcestershire sauce**

1 teaspoon **mild hot sauce**, such as Cholula or Frank's

The crunchiness of *patatas bravas*, the Spanish tapa of crusty potatoes burnished with paprika and served with aioli, is maximized in an air fryer. For these spiralized potatoes, I applied those same flavors, tossing the potatoes with hot paprika for color and flavor, but serving them with a homemade ketchup that's equally great with plain french fries of any size and flavor.

SERVES 2

1. Using a spiralizer, spiralize the potato, then place in a large colander. (If you don't have a spiralizer, cut the potato into thin ⅛-inch-thick matchsticks.) Rinse the potatoes under cold running water until the water runs clear. Spread the potatoes out on a double-thick layer of paper towels and pat completely dry.

2. In a large bowl, combine the potatoes, oil, paprika, and garlic powder. Season with salt and pepper and toss to combine. Transfer the potatoes to the air fryer and cook at 400°F until the potatoes are browned and crisp, 15 minutes, shaking the basket halfway through.

3. Meanwhile, in a small blender, puree the tomatoes, vinegar, brown sugar, Worcestershire, and hot sauce until smooth. Pour into a small saucepan or skillet and simmer over medium heat until reduced by half, 3 to 5 minutes. Pour the homemade ketchup into a bowl and let cool.

4. Remove the spiralized potato nest from the air fryer and serve hot with the ketchup.

ALL-PURPOSE SPICED COCKTAIL NUTS

If you've ever wanted to throw an impromptu
cocktail party after work, all you need
is this ridiculously simple nut mix on
hand that's ready to serve in less than
10 minutes. The nuts fry up crunchy and hot,
the perfect complement to icy-cold cocktails.
You can use 2 cups of any kind of nuts, or,
for a shortcut, pick up a can of mixed nuts
on your way home from work—just use half the
amount of salt here since the mixed nuts
come salted and check them after cooking for
4 minutes to see if they're done since the
canned nuts also come preroasted.

MAKES 2 CUPS

½ cup **raw cashews**

½ cup **raw pecan halves**

½ cup **raw walnut halves**

½ cup **raw whole almonds**

2 tablespoons **olive oil**

1 tablespoon **light brown sugar**

1 teaspoon chopped fresh **rosemary leaves**

1 teaspoon chopped fresh **thyme leaves**

1 teaspoon **kosher salt**

½ teaspoon **ground coriander**

¼ teaspoon **onion powder**

¼ teaspoon **freshly ground black pepper**

⅛ teaspoon **garlic powder**

1. In a large bowl, combine all the ingredients and toss
   until the nuts are evenly coated in the herbs, spices, and
   sugar. Scrape the nuts and seasonings into the air fryer
   and cook at 350°F until golden brown and fragrant, about
   6 minutes, shaking the basket halfway through. Transfer
   the cocktail nuts to a bowl and serve warm.

FRENCH ONION POTATO SKINS

2 small **russet potatoes**, preferably of equal size and shape (about 6 ounces each)

2 teaspoons **olive oil**

Kosher salt and **freshly ground black pepper**

Air-Fried Onions (recipe follows)

1 tablespoon **Worcestershire sauce**

2 teaspoons **sherry vinegar**

2 teaspoons fresh **thyme leaves**, chopped

½ cup grated **Gruyère cheese**

Air-Fried Onions
Makes a little less than 1 cup

1 large **yellow onion**, thinly sliced (about 2 cups)

1 tablespoon **olive oil**

½ teaspoon **kosher salt**

½ teaspoon **sugar**

In a large bowl, toss the onion with the olive oil, salt, and sugar. Transfer to a 7-inch round cake pan insert, metal cake pan, or foil pan, place the pan in the air fryer, and cook at 300°F, stirring every 5 minutes, until browned and crispy and lightly caramelized in parts, 30 to 40 minutes.

Potato skins are a game-night and tailgating favorite for good reason—their crispy fried shells, filled with cheese, sour cream, and bacon, are instantly craveable. For this dinnertime version, I gussied up the populist appetizer with some fried onions and seasonings inspired by French onion soup. The air fryer gets the potato skins exceptionally crisp while the onions, Gruyère cheese, and Worcestershire turn all your favorite parts of the soup into a decadent, handheld bite—no spoon needed.

SERVES 2 TO 4

1. Brush the potatoes with the olive oil and season with salt and pepper. Air fry at 350°F until the potatoes are tender and golden brown, about 40 minutes. Transfer the potatoes to a cutting board and let cool for 5 minutes.

2. Halve the potatoes lengthwise, then use a melon baller, teaspoon, or small spoon to scoop out and discard the potato flesh, leaving a ⅛-inch-thick shell of potato and skin. (If you want to save the potato flesh, mash it while warm with a little olive oil or butter, season with salt and pepper, and refrigerate to serve for dinner another night, for making potato pancakes, or for making hash the next morning for breakfast.)

3. In a small bowl, combine the onions, Worcestershire, vinegar, thyme, and salt and pepper to taste. Divide the mixture among the potato shells. Top them evenly with the Gruyère, then place in the air fryer and cook at 375°F until the cheese is melted and the filling is warmed through, 8 to 10 minutes.

Shortcut:

If you want to have these potato skins even faster, use your microwave! Simply poke the potatoes all over with the tines of a fork, then cook until tender, about 10 minutes on high power. Once cooled slightly, brush the oil on the skin side of the potato shells before filling them and transferring to the air fryer to finish cooking.

CRISPY HERBED CHICKPEAS

1 can (15 ounces) **chickpeas**, rinsed and dried with paper towels

1 tablespoon **olive oil**

½ teaspoon dried **rosemary**

½ teaspoon dried **parsley**

½ teaspoon dried **chives**

¼ teaspoon **mustard powder**

¼ teaspoon **sweet paprika**

¼ teaspoon **cayenne pepper**

Kosher salt and **freshly ground black pepper**

Note:

During testing, I found that different brands of canned chickpeas "fry" up at wildly different rates. Some brands only took 6 minutes to get crisp, while other brands, where the chickpeas were comparatively larger in size and meatier, took almost double that. Hence, the range in cooking time for this recipe. Start out with your favorite go-to brand and cook them for 6 minutes. If they're not crisp enough after that, continue cooking in 2-minute intervals until they are. Then you'll know the correct amount of time for that specific brand.

In my opinion, "crispy chickpeas" never lived up to their promise, and were a constant disappointment when I made them whether they were deep-fried or roasted in the oven. They often came out too soggy and chewy, rather than truly crispy. So I set out to see if the air fryer did a better job. And I can confidently say, it does the best job I've ever witnessed of making *actually* crisp chickpeas. The high heat, circulating at a super-fast speed, dries out the chickpeas so they're almost dehydrated. Be careful, or you'll start eating these and wake up 5 minutes later to an empty bowl.

MAKES 1½ CUPS

1. In a large bowl, combine all the ingredients except the kosher salt and black pepper and toss until the chickpeas are evenly coated in the herbs and spices. Scrape the chickpeas and seasonings into the air fryer and cook at 350°F until browned and crisp, 6 to 12 minutes, shaking the basket halfway through. Transfer the crispy chickpeas to a bowl, sprinkle with kosher salt and black pepper, and serve warm.

MAIN EVENTS

SMOKY CHICKEN PARM SANDWICHES

2 boneless, skinless **chicken breasts** (8 ounces each), sliced horizontally in half and separated into 4 thinner cutlets

Kosher salt and **freshly ground black pepper**

½ cup **all-purpose flour**

3 large **eggs**, lightly beaten

½ cup dried **breadcrumbs**

1 tablespoon **smoked paprika**

Cooking spray

½ cup **marinara sauce**, homemade or store-bought

6 ounces **smoked mozzarella cheese**, grated

2 store-bought soft, **sesame-seed hamburger** or **Italian buns**, split

There's not much you can do to improve upon a chicken parm sandwich in my opinion. The marriage of a fried chicken cutlet, somehow staying crispy while bathed in warm tomato sauce and blanketed in gooey mozzarella cheese, all stuffed inside a soft sesame-seed roll is heaven. But for this air-fried version, I wanted to infuse a bit of my favorite spice, smoked paprika, into the chicken and up the "smoky" flavor with pleasantly pungent smoked mozzarella. It gives the sandwich a certain "wood-fired" quality that's a wonderful change of pace, whether at a barbecue in the summer or a cold cabin during the winter, all without having to strike a match.

SERVES 2

1. Season the chicken cutlets all over with salt and pepper. Set up three shallow bowls: Place the flour in the first bowl, the eggs in the second, and stir together the breadcrumbs and smoked paprika in the third. Coat the chicken pieces in the flour, then dip fully in the egg. Dredge in the paprika breadcrumbs, then transfer to a wire rack set over a baking sheet and spray both sides liberally with cooking spray.

2. Transfer 2 of the chicken cutlets to the air fryer and cook at 350°F until beginning to brown, about 6 minutes. Spread each cutlet with 2 tablespoons of the marinara sauce and sprinkle with one-quarter of the smoked mozzarella. Increase the heat to 400°F and cook until the chicken is cooked through and crisp and the cheese is melted and golden brown, about 5 minutes more.

8. Transfer the cutlets to a plate, stack on top of each other, and place inside a bun. Repeat with the remaining chicken cutlets, marinara, smoked mozzarella, and bun. Serve the sandwiches warm.

HERBED BUTTERMILK ROAST CHICKEN BREAST

Depending on the size of your air fryer, you might fit a whole chicken inside, but some are too small, so I wanted to give a roast chicken recipe that could work in every model and size of machine. Bone-in, skin-on chicken breasts are super flavorful and, in some cases, so large they might as well be a whole chicken. Here I cover them with a spice mix inspired by dry ranch-style seasoning, suffusing the chicken skin with tons of dried herbs and umami-packed onion and garlic. Serve up the chicken in thick slices like a roast chicken or refrigerate and tear it into pieces for chicken salad (the chicken is preseasoned and only needs a little mayonnaise to hold it together).

SERVES 2

1 large bone-in, skin-on **chicken breast** (1¼ to 1½ pounds)

1 cup **buttermilk**

1½ teaspoons dried **parsley**

1½ teaspoons dried **chives**

¾ teaspoon **kosher salt**

½ teaspoon dried **dill**

½ teaspoon **onion powder**

¼ teaspoon **garlic powder**

¼ teaspoon dried **tarragon**

Cooking spray

1. Place the chicken breast in a bowl and pour over the buttermilk, turning the chicken in it to make sure it's completely covered. Let the chicken stand at room temperature for at least 20 minutes or in the refrigerator for up to 4 hours.

2. Meanwhile, in a bowl, stir together the parsley, chives, salt, dill, onion powder, garlic powder, and tarragon.

(recipe continues)

3. Remove the chicken from the buttermilk, letting the excess drip off, then place skin-side up directly in the air fryer. Sprinkle the seasoning mix all over the top of the chicken breast, then let stand until the herb mix soaks into the buttermilk, at least 5 minutes.

4. Spray the top of the chicken with cooking spray. Cook at 300°F for 10 minutes, then increase the heat to 350°F and cook until an instant-read thermometer inserted into the thickest part of the breast reads 160°F and the chicken is deep golden brown, 30 to 35 minutes.

5. Transfer the chicken breast to a cutting board, let rest for 10 minutes, then cut the meat off the bone and cut into thick slices for serving.

THANKSGIVING-LEFTOVER MONTE CRISTO

While I've never gotten the whole idea of taking Thanksgiving leftovers and coming up with new ways to eat them in the post-feast days (I'm too tired to cook MORE), this sandwich is definitely something I can support. To assemble, it only takes the effort that I'd normally put toward microwaving a plate of leftovers, but in the air fryer, I can crisp up the edges and get it all melty and hot without having to stand over the stove or wait for it to cook for 30 minutes in the oven. With a sandwich this delicious and fast, I get it now.

SERVES 1

1. To assemble the sandwich, spread the cranberry sauce on one slice of bread, then layer the mashed potatoes, turkey, green beans, stuffing, and cheese on top of it. Spread the butter on the second slice of bread and place on top of the cheese, butter-side down. Press lightly on the sandwich to compress.

2. In a pie dish, combine the milk and eggs and season with salt and pepper. Dip the sandwich in the custard, flipping to make sure it soaks in both sides, then transfer the sandwich to the air fryer. Cook at 375°F until the sandwich is golden brown and warmed throughout, about 12 minutes.

3. Transfer the sandwich to a cutting board, halve diagonally, and dust with powdered sugar. Serve hot with a small bowl of warmed leftover gravy for dipping.

2 tablespoons **cranberry sauce**

2 thick (1-inch) slices **country white** or **sourdough bread**

½ cup leftover **mashed potatoes**

2 thick slices leftover **cooked turkey breast**

½ cup leftover **cooked green beans**

⅓ cup leftover **stuffing**

2 slices **Swiss cheese**

1 tablespoon **unsalted butter**, at room temperature

½ cup **milk**

2 large **eggs**, lightly beaten

Kosher salt and **freshly ground black pepper**

Powdered sugar, for dusting

⅓ cup leftover **gravy**

Switch It Up:

This sandwich archetype works great with other fillings as well. Instead of mashed potatoes, green beans, and stuffing, substitute cooked bacon and sliced avocado for a club, or leftover roasted veggies and mozzarella. Use whatever leftovers you have to make your favorite combination.

"ORIGINAL RECIPE" FRIED CHICKEN TENDERS

1 pound boneless, skinless **chicken breasts**, cut into 1-inch-thick strips

1 cup **buttermilk**

2 large **eggs**, lightly beaten

1 cup **all-purpose flour**

2 tablespoons **sweet paprika**

1½ tablespoons **ground white pepper**

1 tablespoon **garlic powder**

1 tablespoon **kosher salt**

1½ teaspoons **celery seeds**

1½ teaspoons **mustard powder**

1½ teaspoons **freshly ground black pepper**

1½ teaspoons **ground ginger**

1 teaspoon dried **basil**

1 teaspoon dried **thyme**

½ teaspoon dried **oregano**

Cooking spray

Go Basic:

Don't have all the spices needed for this recipe? Don't worry—just omit them, except the salt, and season the flour with ground black pepper. The plain tenders will taste just as good on their own, especially when dunked in your favorite dipping sauce.

Chicken tenders are fantastic party fare and super kid-friendly, but I rarely think to make them at home for dinner because of the deep-frying. These tenders, however, I could make any night of the week because they're easy to throw together. I based them on a certain fried chicken chain's original recipe chicken. It was my favorite snack as a kid, and through lots of trial and error, I've stumbled upon the right mix of eleven herbs and spices to stand up to the colonel's. Serve these with your favorite dipping sauce or in classic fashion, with sides of mashed potatoes and biscuits (page 28) with gravy.

SERVES 2 TO 4

1. In a large bowl, combine the chicken strips, buttermilk, and eggs and refrigerate for at least 2 hours or up to overnight.

2. Meanwhile, in a bowl, stir together the flour, paprika, white pepper, garlic powder, salt, celery seed, mustard powder, black pepper, ginger, basil, thyme, and oregano.

3. Remove a few strips at a time from the buttermilk mixture, dredge in the seasoned flour until evenly coated, then transfer to a wire rack set over a baking sheet. Spray the chicken strips all over with cooking spray.

4. Transfer half the strips to the air fryer in a single layer and cook at 375°F until golden brown and cooked through, about 8 minutes. Transfer the cooked strips to a plate and repeat to cook the remaining strips. Serve the strips hot.

GARLICKY SOY-GLAZED CHICKEN THIGHS

2 tablespoons **chicken stock**

2 tablespoons **reduced-sodium soy sauce**

1½ tablespoons **sugar**

4 **garlic cloves**, smashed and peeled

2 large **scallions**, cut into 2- to 3-inch batons, plus more, thinly sliced, for garnish

2 bone-in, skin-on **chicken thighs** (7 to 8 ounces each)

No pan insert?

If you don't want to use the pan insert, you can still make these chicken thighs. Simply heat the sauce in the microwave to dissolve the sugar, then brush it over the chicken thighs every 5 minutes, flipping them before you brush, until done. You will have some glaze left over, and the chicken won't have as intense a flavor as if they were cooked in the sauce, but they'll still be glazed, sticky, and crisp on top.

One of my favorite preparations of chicken I've ever eaten was at a Japanese restaurant in New York City that served up chicken thighs, still sizzling on a hot stone, that had been glazed in nothing but sweetened soy sauce and garlic. The condensed marinade was sticky and packed with the flavor of the chicken skin's own rendered fat. I set out to re-create them for the air fryer. Turned a few times while sitting in the marinade, the chicken thighs infuse with the umami glaze and their skins crisp up under the high heat of the air fryer's fan. It creates a crispy, tender, lip-smacking texture that bests the restaurant version.

SERVES 1 OR 2

1. In a 7-inch round cake pan insert, metal cake pan, or foil pan, combine the chicken stock, soy sauce, and sugar and stir until the sugar dissolves. Add the garlic cloves, scallions, and chicken thighs, turning the thighs to coat them in the marinade, then resting them skin-side up. Place the pan in the air fryer and cook at 375°F, flipping the thighs every 5 minutes after the first 10 minutes, until the chicken is cooked through and the marinade is reduced to a sticky glaze over the chicken, about 30 minutes.

2. Remove the pan from the air fryer and serve the chicken thighs warm, with any remaining glaze spooned over top and sprinkled with more sliced scallions.

CHINESE BBQ–STYLE TOFU AND SCALLIONS

7 ounces (½ package) **extra-firm tofu**, drained and cut into slabs ¾ inch thick, 1 inch wide, and 2 inches long

2 tablespoons **reduced-sodium soy sauce**

2 tablespoons **rice vinegar**

1 tablespoon **honey**

1 tablespoon **hoisin sauce**

2 teaspoons **sriracha hot sauce**

1 teaspoon **Chinese five-spice powder**

¼ teaspoon **garlic powder**

Freshly ground black pepper

4 **scallions**, cut into 2-inch batons

Cooked white rice, for serving

No pan insert?

If you don't want to use the pan insert, you can still make this tofu. Simply brush the tofu pieces with the sauce every 5 minutes, flipping them before you brush, until done. You will have some glaze left over, and the tofu won't have as intense a flavor as if it had been cooked in the sauce, but it'll still be glazed and sticky.

Char siu pork is one of my favorite dishes, but the pork belly it's made with means it's only a rare indulgence. To make the dish healthier and more weeknight-friendly, I decided to apply the same sticky, savory-sweet glaze to tofu, which transforms the otherwise bland bean curd into umami bombs that are addictive to eat over rice. The glaze is packed with flavor thanks to a mix of soy sauce, honey, sriracha, and Chinese five-spice powder. Glaze pieces of chicken, pork, or your shoe, really, in this sauce, and it will taste wonderful, trust me.

SERVES 2

1. Place the tofu slabs between sheets of paper towels, top with a heavy board or skillet, and let stand for 15 minutes to absorb any excess moisture.

2. Meanwhile, in a bowl, whisk together the soy sauce, vinegar, honey, hoisin, sriracha, five-spice powder, garlic powder, and black pepper to taste until smooth.

3. Place the tofu pieces and scallions in a 7-inch round cake pan insert, metal cake pan, or foil pan and pour the sauce over them, turning the tofu to coat in sauce. Place the pan in the air fryer and cook at 375°F, turning the tofu every 5 minutes, until the sauce is reduced and glazed over the tofu and scallions, about 18 minutes. Remove the pan from the air fryer and serve the tofu and scallions hot over rice.

MANCHURIAN-STYLE CHICKEN

No one is quite sure where this dish came
from, nor why it's called what it is, but
this Chinese-inspired dish of chicken breast
pieces cooked up in a slightly sweet, umami-
packed, spicy sauce is one of the more
surprising and satisfying chicken dishes I've
ever had. And because the chicken cooks in
the sauce, it's a virtual one-bowl dinner
that, if you prep the morning of, can mean
dinner is on the table quicker than it takes
to slip on your most comfortable socks and
queue up a good Netflix show.

SERVES 2

1. In a bowl, combine the chicken, ketchup, chili sauce, soy
   sauce, vinegar, oil, hot sauce, garlic powder, cayenne, and
   three-quarters of the scallions and toss until evenly coated.

2. Scrape the chicken and sauce into a 7-inch round cake
   pan insert, metal cake pan, or foil pan and place the pan
   in the air fryer. Cook at 350°F until the chicken is cooked
   through and the sauce is reduced to a thick glaze, about
   20 minutes, flipping the chicken pieces halfway through.

3. Remove the pan from the air fryer. Spoon the chicken and
   sauce over rice and top with the remaining scallions.

1 pound boneless, skinless
chicken breasts, cut into
1-inch pieces

¼ cup **ketchup**

1 tablespoon **tomato-
based chili sauce**, such
as Heinz

1 tablespoon **soy sauce**

1 tablespoon **rice vinegar**

2 teaspoons **vegetable oil**

1 teaspoon **hot sauce**, such
as Tabasco

½ teaspoon **garlic powder**

¼ teaspoon **cayenne
pepper**

2 **scallions**, thinly sliced

Cooked white rice, for
serving

PORK SCHNITZEL WITH ROAST POTATO AND CUCUMBER SALAD

Crispy pork schnitzel doesn't need to be fried in loads of oil, splattering all over your stove, to be traditional or delicious. This air-fried version bakes up super crisp and quick, making it ideal for a weeknight dinner. Traditionally, it's served with buttered potatoes and cucumbers in yogurt. I streamlined the process here, roasting the potatoes, then tossing them with the cucumbers and yogurt while warm so they soak up the dressing and become a creamy, warm potato salad.

SERVES 2

1. In a large bowl, toss the potatoes with the oil and season with salt and pepper. Transfer the potatoes to the air fryer and cook at 375°F until the potatoes are tender, 15 to 20 minutes, shaking the basket halfway through. Transfer the potatoes to a cutting board and let cool enough to handle.

2. Place the flour, eggs, and breadcrumbs in three separate shallow bowls. Dredge the cutlets in the flour, then the egg, then the breadcrumbs and season with salt and pepper.

3. Spray the breaded cutlets liberally with cooking spray. Transfer 2 cutlets to the air fryer and cook at 375°F until the breading is golden brown, about 8 minutes. Transfer to a plate and repeat with the remaining cutlets.

4. Slice the potatoes into thick coins, then toss in a bowl with the yogurt, dill, cucumber, and garlic and season with salt and pepper. Divide the salad between the plates and serve with the warm schnitzel topped with more dill.

¾ pound **fingerling potatoes**

1 tablespoon **vegetable oil**

Kosher salt and **freshly ground black pepper**

1 cup **all-purpose flour**

3 large **eggs**, lightly beaten

1 cup **panko breadcrumbs**

2 boneless top **pork loin chops** (5 ounces each), halved horizontally into 4 thinner cutlets

Cooking spray

¼ cup **plain Greek yogurt**

1 tablespoon finely chopped fresh **dill**, plus more for garnish

1 small or ½ medium **cucumber**, peeled, seeded, and thinly sliced

1 **garlic clove**, minced

Switch It Up:

You can substitute four 2½-ounce chicken or veal cutlets for the pork here, and cook as directed.

CIDER-BRINED
MUSTARD PORK CHOPS

2 cups **apple cider**

¼ cup **kosher salt**

¼ cup packed **light brown sugar**

2 boneless top **pork loin chops,** ½ inch thick (4 to 6 ounces each)

Freshly ground black pepper

1 cup **panko breadcrumbs**

1 tablespoon chopped fresh **thyme leaves**

1 tablespoon chopped fresh **rosemary leaves**

¼ cup **Dijon mustard**

Cooking spray

Apple is a classic pairing for pork, and here it infuses boneless pork chops via a cider brine, which makes the meat extra moist. The chops are coated in sharp Dijon mustard and then in crispy breadcrumbs, making them an elegant weeknight meal with roasted apples and sautéed cabbage.

SERVES 2

1. In a large plastic container, whisk together the cider, salt, and brown sugar until the salt and sugar dissolve. Submerge the pork chops in the brine and refrigerate for at least 2 hours or up to overnight.

2. Drain and rinse the pork chops, pat them completely dry with paper towels, then season them with pepper. On a shallow plate, combine the breadcrumbs, thyme, and rosemary. Brush or smear the mustard all over the pork chops, then crust them in the herbed breadcrumbs and place them on a wire rack.

3. Spray the pork chops liberally with cooking spray. Place the chops in the air fryer and cook at 350°F until golden brown and the pork is cooked through, 10 to 12 minutes.

4. Transfer the pork chops to plates and serve warm.

CHILE-RUBBED RIB EYE

There are a couple of essential rules to making a great steak in the air fryer. First, make sure the steak is fully at room temperature before you cook it so that the temperature shock from the air fryer doesn't cause the meat to seize up and tighten more than it naturally does. And second, rub the steak with a flavorful dry rub to give the outside color and flavor. Feel free to try out other spice mixes or rubs that you like, and if you want to keep it simple, go with lots of salt and coarsely ground black pepper and the steak will still come out perfect, no extra pans or grill required.

SERVES 2

1½ teaspoons **chili powder**

1½ teaspoons **ground espresso**

1½ teaspoons **dark brown sugar**

1 teaspoon **sweet paprika**

½ teaspoon **kosher salt**

½ teaspoon **freshly ground black pepper**

1 **rib eye steak** (1 to 1¼ pounds), 1¼ inches thick, at room temperature

1. In a small bowl, combine the chili powder, ground espresso, brown sugar, paprika, salt, and pepper. Sprinkle it evenly over the steak, rubbing it into both sides. Let the steak stand for at least 10 minutes, if you have the time.

2. Transfer it to the air fryer and cook at 400°F until browned on the outside and cooked to medium-rare, 10 to 12 minutes. To make sure your steak is cooked to your desired doneness, insert an instant-read thermometer lengthwise through the steak and continue cooking until your desired temperature is reached; 135°F is perfect for medium-rare.

3. Transfer the steak to a cutting board and let rest for at least 10 minutes. Slice the steak across the grain and serve warm.

JAMAICAN BEEF MEATBALLS WITH LIME-COCONUT YOGURT

1 pound **ground beef**, at room temperature

⅓ cup **dried breadcrumbs**

3 tablespoons **curry powder**

2 tablespoons fresh **thyme leaves**, chopped

1 teaspoon **ground allspice**

Kosher salt and **freshly ground black pepper**

1 small **yellow onion**, grated on a box grater

1 **Scotch bonnet** or **habanero chile**, seeded and minced

½ cup **coconut yogurt** (or dairy yogurt)

1 tablespoon finely chopped fresh **cilantro**

Finely grated **zest and juice of ½ lime**

Any time I'm in a Caribbean neighborhood, I love stopping by a local corner deli or restaurant to get a Jamaican beef patty-like a savory, stuffed hand pie-warm from the fryer. These meatballs-the patty without the crust, if you will-are teeming with spices like curry powder, allspice, and thyme and fresh Scotch bonnet chile (feel free to add as much as you can take, if you're a spice lover). Served with a cooling lime-coconut yogurt, these just might be my favorite new party snack-or as a full meal, served over rice to help soak up all the delicious, flavorful juices.

MAKES 16 MEATBALLS

1. In a large bowl, combine the beef, breadcrumbs, curry powder, thyme, allspice, 1 teaspoon salt, ½ teaspoon pepper, the grated onion, and the chile and mix with your hands (wear gloves if your skin is sensitive to chiles!) until the mixture is evenly incorporated. Divide the mixture into 16 portions and roll each one into a ball.

2. Transfer the meatballs to the air fryer in a single layer and cook at 350°F, shaking the basket halfway through, until golden brown on the outside and no longer pink in the middle, about 15 minutes.

3. In a small bowl, whisk together the yogurt, cilantro, lime zest, and lime juice and season with salt and pepper.

4. Transfer the meatballs to plates and serve hot with the lime-coconut yogurt sauce.

CHIPOTLE CARNE ASADA TACOS

Flank or skirt steak for carne asada tacos is traditionally marinated in lots of orange juice to tenderize and flavor the meat. For this air-fried version, however, I swapped in the non-wet versions of its flavorings so the steak can cook up in the air fryer with a crisp, flavorful exterior. Chipotle chile powder is available online, if not in your local grocery, and pairs beautifully with fresh orange zest in this spice rub. Once cooked, thinly slice the steak and serve up authentic-ish carne asada tacos at home without the need for a grill.

SERVES 2 TO 4

1 tablespoon **chili powder**

2 teaspoons **chipotle chile powder**

1 teaspoon **kosher salt**

1 teaspoon **garlic powder**

Finely grated **zest of 1 orange**

1 tablespoon **vegetable oil**

1 pound **flank steak** (¾ inch thick), at room temperature

Corn tortillas, avocado slices, diced white onion, cilantro leaves, and **salsa,** for serving

1. In a small bowl, stir together the chili powder, chipotle powder, salt, garlic powder, and orange zest. Working on a plate, rub the spice mix all over the steak, then drizzle it with the oil, turning the steak so the oil coats it evenly. Place the steak in the air fryer and cook at 400°F until browned on the outside and medium-rare inside, about 10 minutes.

2. Transfer the steak to a cutting board and let stand for at least 10 minutes. Thinly slice the steak across the grain and serve in warm tortillas, topped with avocado, onion, cilantro, and your favorite salsa.

CORIANDER-CRUSTED ROAST BEEF

2 tablespoons **coriander seeds**

1 tablespoon **black peppercorns**

3 tablespoons **vegetable oil**

1 tablespoon **kosher salt**

1 (2-pound) trimmed **beef top sirloin roast**, tied, at room temperature

---

Switch It Up:

This method of cooking beef works no matter what the flavorings are on the outside, so if you don't have coriander or don't like the flavor, simply leave it off or substitute another crushed seed like fennel seeds, cumin seeds, or white and pink peppercorns.

This recipe is, perhaps, the one I'm most proud of because it's so impressive. Instead of spending hours in an oven, air fry a sirloin roast, here crusted in crushed coriander seeds and black peppercorns, and have perfectly cooked roast beef ready for guests in about an hour. Even better, save the whole roast or any leftovers for later to make deli-style roast beef sandwiches (it's much easier to get thin slices once the beef is chilled).

SERVES 6 TO 8

1. Combine the coriander seeds and peppercorns in plastic bag and crush with a heavy skillet or rolling pin until just cracked open (or use a mortar and pestle). Mix in the oil and salt and stir to form a spice paste. Spread the paste evenly all over the beef.

2. Transfer the beef roast to the air fryer and cook at 325°F, turning the roast every 10 minutes, until golden brown and an instant-read thermometer inserted into the middle of the roast reads 125° to 130°F, about 40 minutes. This temperature is for medium-rare doneness, the ideal temperature for roast beef.

3. Transfer the beef roast to a cutting board and let rest for at least 15 minutes. Cut the beef into thick slices and serve warm. If not eating right away or to make sandwiches, wrap the cooled roast in plastic wrap and refrigerate until firm to help in getting thin slices of meat, at least 4 hours and up to 5 days.

SPICY ORANGE-GLAZED BEEF

½ pound trimmed **beef sirloin**, cut into strips 1 inch long and ½ inch wide

3 tablespoons **orange marmalade**

Finely grated **zest of ½ orange**

1 tablespoon fresh **orange juice**

1 tablespoon **vegetable oil**

1 tablespoon **soy sauce**

1 teaspoon **cornstarch**

1 teaspoon **mild hot sauce**, such as Frank's

½ teaspoon **garlic powder**

Freshly ground black pepper

Cooked white rice, for serving

I love Chinese takeout just as much as the next person, but sometimes it's nice to prepare the dish at home to make it healthier, which allows me to eat more of it! My favorite combination is tender strips of beef coated in a sweet, slightly bitter orange sauce. The Chinese take-out versions often use orange extract to drive home the orange flavor, but here, I lean on orange marmalade, orange zest, and orange juice to imbue the beef with their bright flavors. The beef cooks up in the sauce until it's reduced and glazed all over—the perfect quick weeknight meal to serve over rice.

SERVES 2

1. In a bowl, combine the beef, orange marmalade, orange zest, orange juice, oil, soy sauce, cornstarch, hot sauce, and garlic powder, season with pepper, and toss until evenly coated. Scrape the beef and sauce into a 7-inch round cake or pizza pan insert, metal cake pan, or foil pan.

2. Place the pan in the air fryer and cook at 375°F until the beef is cooked through and the sauce is reduced to a thick glaze, about 10 minutes, stirring halfway through. Remove the pan from the air fryer and spoon the beef and sauce over rice to serve.

BLACKENED RED SNAPPER

When I was growing up in the South in the '90s, blackened red snapper was the trendy fish preparation, especially in and around New Orleans, where it was popularized by the legendary chef Paul Prudhomme. Most everyone used Chef Paul's store-bought, premade blackening seasoning, and it's good, but it never hurts to have a from-scratch recipe ready to go for when you want to control the type and amount of spices. This is my take, put to good use in this air-fried version, which cooks up moist and is enjoyed with a cooling, tangy rémoulade sauce. Serve it up over cooked grits or roasted potatoes for a simple take on this old-school NOLA classic.

SERVES 1 OR 2

1. In a bowl, stir together the paprika, salt, onion powder, garlic powder, cayenne, black pepper, oregano, and thyme. Rub 2 teaspoons of the oil all over each fillet, then sprinkle both fillets all over with the dry seasonings.

2. Place 1 fillet, skin-side down, in the air fryer and cook at 375°F until the fish is just cooked through, about 6 minutes. Use a long, thin spatula to transfer the cooked fillet to a plate and repeat with the second fillet.

3. Meanwhile, make the rémoulade: In a small bowl, whisk together the mayonnaise, mustard, ketchup, hot sauce, Worcestershire, salt, cayenne, and garlic until smooth.

4. Serve the fillets with a dollop of the rémoulade sauce.

1½ teaspoons **sweet paprika**

1 teaspoon **kosher salt**

½ teaspoon **onion powder**

½ teaspoon **garlic powder**

½ teaspoon **cayenne pepper**

½ teaspoon **freshly ground black pepper**

½ teaspoon dried **oregano**

½ teaspoon dried **thyme**

4 teaspoons **vegetable oil**

2 **red snapper fillets** (½ pound each)

For the rémoulade sauce:

½ cup **mayonnaise**

3 tablespoons **spicy brown mustard**

1 tablespoon **ketchup**

1 teaspoon **hot sauce**, such as Tabasco

1 teaspoon **Worcestershire sauce**

½ teaspoon **kosher salt**

⅛ teaspoon **cayenne pepper**

1 **garlic clove**, grated on a Microplane grater

Switch It Up:

Any thin, firm-fleshed fish fillet can take the place of the snapper here. Skate, flounder, or trout make great alternatives.

TANDOORI-SPICED
SALMON AND POTATOES

Inspired by a recipe from Madhur Jaffrey, an
Indian cookbook legend, salmon fillets are
rubbed in fragrant, warming tandoori spices,
a perfect match for the fish's rich flavor.
The salmon is then roasted atop fingerling
potatoes, and thanks to the efficiency of the
air fryer, they'll be ready at the same time.
It's the perfect one-air fryer meal.

SERVES 2

1 pound **fingerling potatoes**

2 tablespoons **vegetable oil**

Kosher salt and **freshly ground black pepper**

1 teaspoon ground **turmeric**

1 teaspoon ground **cumin**

1 teaspoon ground **ginger**

½ teaspoon **smoked paprika**

¼ teaspoon **cayenne pepper**

2 skin-on **salmon fillets** (6 ounces each)

1. In a bowl, toss the potatoes with 1 tablespoon of the oil until evenly coated. Season with salt and pepper. Transfer the potatoes to the air fryer and cook at 375°F for 20 minutes.

2. Meanwhile, in a bowl, combine the remaining 1 tablespoon oil, the turmeric, cumin, ginger, paprika, and cayenne. Add the salmon fillets and turn in the spice mixture until fully coated all over.

3. After the potatoes have cooked 20 minutes, place the salmon fillets, skin-side up, on top of the potatoes, and continue cooking until the potatoes are tender, the salmon is cooked, and the salmon skin is slightly crisp, 5 to 8 minutes for medium to well-done.

4. Transfer the salmon fillets to two plates and serve with the potatoes while both are warm.

CORNMEAL-CRUSTED TROUT FINGERS WITH TARTAR SAUCE

½ cup **yellow cornmeal**, medium or finely ground (not coarse)

⅓ cup **all-purpose flour**

1½ teaspoons **baking powder**

1 teaspoon **kosher salt**, plus more as needed

½ teaspoon **freshly ground black pepper**, plus more as needed

⅛ teaspoon **cayenne pepper**

¾ pound skinless **trout fillets**, cut into strips 1 inch wide and 3 inches long

3 large **eggs**, lightly beaten

Cooking spray

½ cup **mayonnaise**

2 tablespoons **capers**, rinsed and finely chopped

1 tablespoon fresh **tarragon**

1 teaspoon fresh **lemon juice**, plus lemon wedges, for serving

Fish sticks are a fried classic, but they're often not made with the best fish. Making your own (admit it, you love 'em) in the air fryer allows you to control the quality of the fish and make them healthier in the process. I like trout for their clean flavor and small size, but feel free to use any white-fleshed fish you want, such as catfish, tilapia, or even swordfish. If the fish can be cut into a finger shape, it works here.

SERVES 2

1. In a large bowl, whisk together the cornmeal, flour, baking powder, salt, black pepper, and cayenne. Dip the trout strips in the egg, then toss them in the cornmeal mixture until fully coated. Transfer the trout to a rack set over a baking sheet and liberally spray all over with cooking spray.

2. Transfer half the fish to the air fryer and cook at 400°F until the fish is cooked through and golden brown, about 6 minutes. Transfer the fish sticks to a plate and repeat with the remaining fish.

3. Meanwhile, in a bowl, whisk together the mayonnaise, capers, tarragon, and lemon juice. Season the tartar sauce with salt and black pepper.

4. Serve the trout fingers hot along with the tartar sauce and lemon wedges.

TOASTED COUSCOUS AND LEMON WITH CUCUMBERS AND FETA

Couscous is already quick to make, which is why I'm always surprised that it's not used more often for weeknight dinners. But as great as couscous is on its own, it's even better when crisped up in the air fryer. It transforms the pasta into a chewy, crunchy grain that stands up to this bright, acidic dressing and fresh vegetables inspired by a Greek salad. Once assembled, the salad stands up over a couple of days in the refrigerator, so it's great to make ahead of time for your weekly lunch meal prep.

SERVES 1 OR 2

½ **lemon**

1 cup cooked and cooled **pearl couscous** (from ½ cup dry)

2 tablespoons **olive oil**

Kosher salt and **freshly ground black pepper**

2 tablespoons **red wine vinegar**

12 **cherry tomatoes**, halved

1 small **shallot**, thinly sliced

¼ medium **cucumber**, roughly chopped

2 ounces **feta cheese**, broken into large crumbles

1 tablespoon roughly chopped fresh **dill**

1. Cut off two ¼-inch-thick slices from the cut side of the lemon half and remove the seeds. (Set the rest of the lemon aside.) Finely chop the slices, then combine them with the couscous and olive oil in a bowl. Season with salt and pepper and toss to coat evenly in the oil.

2. Transfer the couscous to a 7-inch round cake pan insert, metal cake pan, or foil pan and reserve the bowl. Place the pan in the air fryer and cook at 350°F, stirring every 5 minutes, until lightly toasted and crunchy, about 20 minutes.

3. Return the hot couscous to the reserved bowl and toss with the vinegar, tomatoes, shallot, and cucumber. Finely grate the zest of the reserved lemon piece over the couscous and season with salt and pepper. Toss to combine, then top the salad with the feta and dill before serving.

GENERAL TSO'S
BROCCOLI "FRIED" RICE

2 cups cooked and cooled **white rice**

1 cup **broccoli florets** (4 ounces)

1 tablespoon plus 2 teaspoons **vegetable oil**

1 teaspoon **toasted sesame oil**

Kosher salt and **freshly ground black pepper**

1 cup **vegetable stock**

4½ tablespoons **rice vinegar**

4½ tablespoons **tomato paste**

3 tablespoons **soy sauce**

1 tablespoon finely grated **garlic**

1 tablespoon finely grated fresh **ginger**

2 teaspoons **cornstarch**

¾ teaspoon crushed **red chile flakes**

Fried rice is the quintessential leftovers dish, but sometimes you don't want to handle the wok and all the prep and dishes that come with it. The air fryer still gives you exceptionally crispy rice, but without all the stirring, flipping, and heating up your kitchen with a high-heat flame. The rice and broccoli toast up super crunchy and then get drizzled with a quick General Tso's-style sauce. Use the leftover sauce as a condiment on sandwiches or as a dip for fried chicken and french fries.

SERVES 1 OR 2

1. In a bowl, combine the rice, broccoli, vegetable oil, and sesame oil. Season with salt and pepper and toss to coat evenly in the oils. Transfer to a 7-inch round cake pan insert, metal cake pan, or foil pan.

2. Place the pan in the air fryer and cook at 350°F, stirring every 5 minutes, until lightly toasted and crunchy, about 12 minutes.

3. Meanwhile, in a small saucepan, combine the stock, vinegar, tomato paste, soy sauce, garlic, ginger, cornstarch, and chile flakes. Bring to a simmer, then cook until reduced and thickened, about 5 minutes. Remove the pan from the heat and let the sauce cool while the rice and broccoli cook.

4. Remove the pan from the air fryer and divide the rice and broccoli between bowls, then drizzle with some of the sauce. Save any remaining sauce in an airtight container in the refrigerator for up to 2 weeks.

CRISPY QUINOA, MUSHROOM, AND PEAR SALAD **WITH FRIED HERBS**

Chewy quinoa is transformed into crisp, crunchy bits in the air fryer. They pair perfectly with tender mushrooms, chopped Asian pear, and hearty herbs like mint and sage, which all make this a decidedly wintery salad, perfect as a side dish, or light salad for lunch. As with all grains that you want to fry, make sure they are cooled and dried thoroughly before frying to ensure they get as crispy as possible.

SERVES 1 OR 2

1. In a bowl, combine the quinoa, mushrooms, olive oil, and salt and pepper to taste and toss to coat evenly in the oil. Transfer to a 7-inch round cake pan insert, metal cake pan, or foil pan and reserve the bowl.

2. Place in the air fryer and cook at 350°F, stirring every 5 minutes and stirring the chile flakes, sage, and garlic into the quinoa during the last 5 minutes of cooking, until lightly toasted and crunchy, about 20 minutes.

3. Return the hot quinoa to the bowl and toss with the lemon juice, parsley, mint, and pear. Season with salt and pepper, then top the salad with the goat cheese before serving.

1 cup cooked and cooled **quinoa**

1 cup quartered **cremini mushrooms** (about 4)

2 tablespoons **olive oil**

Kosher salt and **freshly ground black pepper**

¼ teaspoon crushed **red chile flakes**

2 fresh **sage leaves**, thinly sliced

1 **garlic clove**, grated on a Microplane grater

2 tablespoons fresh **lemon juice**

1 tablespoon roughly chopped fresh **flat-leaf parsley leaves**

4 large fresh **mint leaves**, thinly sliced

½ **Asian pear**, peeled, cored, and cut into ¼-inch-thick slices

2 ounces **goat cheese**, crumbled

VEGETABLES

HOW TO AIR FRY ANY VEGETABLE

Air fryers are particularly adept at cooking most vegetables with a pleasing, lightly blistered or caramelized exterior, while being perfectly tender inside. Never worry about spreading out vegetables on a big baking sheet and heating up the oven again, because the air fryer does a better job. It also comes in handy when you're already pan-frying steak, chicken, or fish on the stove. Your meal-prep time will also be considerably shortened now with all these vegetables to air fry in an instant. The ultimate game-changers, though? The easiest roasted garlic and kale chips you've ever made.

Get started with these vegetables in the chart opposite by simply tossing each in a bowl with just enough oil to coat and salt and pepper to taste. Place them in the air fryer basket and cook using the temperatures and cook times listed until lightly browned and tender. Serve as is or finish them with one of the five all-purpose toppings that follow on page 100. Or feel free to serve them with your own favorite sauces or any of the condiments paired with the other vegetables in this chapter. With so many delicious options, you won't get tired of ways to enjoy them.

VEGETABLE (about ½ pound)	PREP	COOK TIME
Asparagus	Ends trimmed and left whole or large spears cut into 2-inch lengths	375°F for 10 minutes
Beets (small)	Leave whole; peel after cooking	375°F for 20 minutes
Bell peppers	Stemmed and seeded, cut into 1-inch-wide strips or squares	375°F for 10 minutes
Broccoli	Broken into 1-inch-wide florets	375°F for 10 minutes
Brussels sprouts	Trimmed, left whole if small, halved if large	375°F for 20 minutes
Butternut/Acorn squash	Peeled and cut into 1-inch cubes	400°F for 15 minutes
Cabbage	Cored and cut into 1-inch-thick wedges	375°F for 15 to 20 minutes
Carrots	Cut into ½-inch pieces	400°F for 15 minutes
Cauliflower	Broken into 1-inch-wide florets	375°F for 10 minutes
Celery root	Peeled and cut into 1-inch cubes	375°F for 15 minutes
Chiles	Stemmed and seeded, cut into 1-inch-wide strips	375°F for 10 minutes
Eggplant	Peeled (optional) and cut into 1-inch cubes	400°F for 15 minutes, stirring every 5 minutes
Fennel	Cut into 1-inch-thick wedges	375°F for 15 minutes
Garlic	Whole cloves, separated, skin-on; squeeze out of skins once cooked	325°F for 10 minutes
Green beans	Ends trimmed and left whole	375°F for 10 minutes
Kale/Collard/Swiss chard (2 to 3 ounces, for kale chips)	Stems and tough ribs removed, torn into 3- to 4-inch pieces	375°F for 4 to 6 minutes
Kohlrabi	Peeled and cut into 1-inch cubes	400°F for 15 minutes
Mushrooms	Left whole, halved or quartered if large	375°F for 12 to 15 minutes
Okra	Left whole, large pods halved lengthwise	400°F for 16 minutes
Parsnips	Peeled and cut into 1-inch cubes	400°F for 15 minutes
Onions	Peeled and cut into 1-inch-thick wedges	375°F for 15 minutes
Potatoes, russet	Peeled (optional) and cut into 1-inch cubes	375°F for 15 minutes
Radishes	Left whole, halved if large	375°F for 10 minutes
Rutabaga	Peeled and cut into 1-inch cubes	400°F for 15 minutes
Sweet potatoes	Peeled (optional) and cut into 1-inch cubes	400°F for 15 minutes
Turnips	Peeled and cut into 1-inch cubes	375°F for 12 minutes
Zucchini/Summer squashes	Cut into 1-inch cubes	375°F for 10 to 12 minutes

How to Finish

Here are five ways to finish your air-fried vegetables. Make them all and store them in airtight containers in your fridge so you can grab them in a flash and jazz up your favorite vegetables whenever the craving hits.

LEMONY TOASTED BREADCRUMBS (GREMOLATA):

Combine 2 cups panko breadcrumbs and ¼ cup olive oil in a large skillet and heat over medium-high heat, tossing and stirring occasionally, until golden brown and toasted, 8 to 10 minutes. Scrape the crumbs into a bowl and stir in ¼ cup finely chopped fresh flat-leaf parsley and the finely grated zest of 1 lemon. Season with salt and pepper and let cool to room temperature. Store the breadcrumbs in an airtight container in the refrigerator for up to 1 week.

Try It On: *bell peppers, potatoes, summer squash*

CITRUS-CHILE OIL:

Using a vegetable peeler, peel off the zest from 1 orange and 1 lemon in large strips. Place them in a small saucepan and pour in 1 cup olive oil or your favorite neutral-flavored oil, 1 tablespoon whole black peppercorns, and 2 dried chiles de árbol. Heat the oil over medium heat until the citrus strips start sizzling, then remove the pan from the heat and let the oil cool to room temperature. Strain out the aromatics, if you like, before storing the oil in the refrigerator for up to 1 week.

Try It On: *broccoli, fennel, rutabaga*

MUSTARD VINAIGRETTE:

In a pint-size mason jar or other resealable container, combine 1 cup olive oil, ⅓ cup white or red wine vinegar, 1 tablespoon plain Dijon mustard, and 1 tablespoon whole-grain Dijon mustard. Season liberally with salt and pepper, then screw on the lid and shake the jar until the dressing is emulsified. Store the vinaigrette in an airtight container in the refrigerator for up to 1 week.

Try It On: *asparagus, mushrooms, onions*

GARLIC YOGURT SAUCE:

Grate 2 small cloves of garlic on a Microplane grater into a bowl and stir in 1 tablespoon fresh lemon juice. Let stand for 1 minute (to allow the lemon juice to soften the bite of the raw garlic), then stir in 1 cup plain Greek yogurt and season with salt and pepper. Store the sauce in an airtight container in the refrigerator for up to 1 week.

Try It On: *beets, eggplant, okra*

HERB PESTO:

Combine 2 cups packed roughly chopped fresh flat-leaf parsley leaves and stems, ½ cup grated parmesan cheese, ⅓ cup pine nuts, and 2 garlic cloves in a small blender or food processor and, with the motor running, slowly pour in ½ cup olive oil until a smooth sauce forms. Season the pesto with salt and pepper, then scrape into an airtight container. Pour over just enough olive oil to cover the top of the pesto in a thin film, then store in the refrigerator for up to 1 week.

Try It On: *cauliflower, green beans, turnips*

MOLE-BRAISED CAULIFLOWER

Some people may scoff at making a mole in less than 10 minutes—and I'm by no means comparing this one to the slow-simmered, traditional moles of Puebla—but for a weeknight meal, it hits all the right spicy-sweet-nutty notes that you'd want from a mole sauce. The cauliflower gets a head start in the air fryer to make sure the florets are tender by the time the sauce comes into play, then it's only 5 minutes more until dinner. Serve this with cooked rice and additions like avocado, rice and beans, and sour cream for a burrito bowl or divided between tortillas for tacos.

SERVES 2

8 ounces medium **cauliflower florets**

1 tablespoon **vegetable oil**

Kosher salt and **freshly ground black pepper**

1½ cups **vegetable broth**

2 tablespoons **New Mexico chile powder** (or regular chili powder)

2 tablespoons **salted roasted peanuts**

1 tablespoon **toasted sesame seeds**, plus more for garnish

1 tablespoon finely chopped **golden raisins**

1 teaspoon **kosher salt**

1 teaspoon **dark brown sugar**

½ teaspoon dried **oregano**

¼ teaspoon **cayenne pepper**

⅛ teaspoon **ground cinnamon**

1. In a large bowl, toss the cauliflower with the oil and season with salt and black pepper. Transfer to a 7-inch round cake pan insert, metal cake pan, or foil pan. Place the pan in the air fryer and cook at 375°F until the cauliflower is tender and lightly browned at the edges, about 10 minutes, stirring halfway through.

2. Meanwhile, in a small blender, combine the broth, chile powder, peanuts, sesame seeds, raisins, salt, brown sugar, oregano, cayenne, and cinnamon and puree until smooth. Pour into a small saucepan or skillet and bring to a simmer over medium heat, then cook until reduced by half, 3 to 5 minutes.

3. Pour the hot mole sauce over the cauliflower in the pan, stir to coat, then cook until the sauce is thickened and lightly charred on the cauliflower, about 5 minutes more. Sprinkle with more sesame seeds and serve warm.

HASSELBACK POTATOES
WITH SOUR CREAM AND CHIVE PESTO

Since the air fryer cooks potatoes exceptionally well, rendering the skins uber crispy, Hasselback potatoes are a natural for the machine. The slices of potato cook up like a standing potato gratin, with plenty of grooves to absorb the sharp chive pesto and dollops of sour cream. It's like an old-school baked potato dressed up in way less time than ever before.

SERVES 2

1. Place the potatoes on a cutting board and lay a chopstick or thin-handled wooden spoon to the side of each potato. Thinly slice the potatoes crosswise, letting the chopstick or spoon handle stop the blade of your knife, and stop ½ inch short of each end of the potato. Rub the potatoes with 1 tablespoon of the olive oil and season with salt and pepper.

2. Place the potatoes, cut-side up, in the air fryer and cook at 375°F until golden brown and crisp on the outside and tender inside, about 40 minutes, drizzling the insides with 1 tablespoon more olive oil and seasoning with more salt and pepper halfway through.

3. Meanwhile, in a small blender or food processor, combine the remaining 3 tablespoons olive oil, the chives, parsley, walnuts, parmesan, lemon juice, and garlic and puree until smooth. Season the chive pesto with salt and pepper.

4. Remove the potatoes from the air fryer and transfer to plates. Drizzle the potatoes with the pesto, letting it drip down into the grooves, then dollop each with sour cream and serve hot.

2 medium **russet potatoes** (8 to 10 ounces each)

5 tablespoons **olive oil**

Kosher salt and **freshly ground black pepper**

¼ cup roughly chopped fresh **chives**

2 tablespoons packed fresh **flat-leaf parsley leaves**

1 tablespoon chopped **walnuts**

1 tablespoon grated **parmesan cheese**

1 teaspoon fresh **lemon juice**

1 small **garlic clove**, peeled

¼ cup **sour cream**

Switch It Up.

Flavor the outside of the potatoes with your favorite dried herbs or spice mix and serve them with your favorite toppings. For a Tex-Mex spin, spice the outside of the potatoes with cumin and coriander, then serve them with salsa, guacamole, and sour cream. Or for a new-fangled loaded potato, serve the potatoes with cooked bacon stuffed into the cuts and topped with grated cheddar, sliced scallions, and a dollop of sour cream topped with chopped chives.

CAESAR WHOLE CAULIFLOWER

3 tablespoons **olive oil**

2 tablespoons **red wine vinegar**

2 tablespoons **Worcestershire sauce**

2 tablespoons grated **parmesan cheese**

1 tablespoon **Dijon mustard**

4 **garlic cloves**, minced

4 **oil-packed anchovy fillets**, drained and finely minced

Kosher salt and **freshly ground black pepper**

1 small head **cauliflower** (about 1 pound), green leaves trimmed and stem trimmed flush with the bottom of the head

1 tablespoon roughly chopped fresh **flat-leaf parsley** (optional)

Go Basic:

If you want to cook a plain roasted whole cauliflower, simply rub it with the olive oil, season all over with salt and pepper, and cook at 340°F for 30 minutes.

Whole roasted cauliflower has, for me anyway, transcended its fad stage, remaining a go-to for an impressive weeknight dinner. Its relatively bland flavor is a perfect canvas for strong, bold additions, like this Caesar salad dressing-inspired marinade. Made with Worcestershire sauce, Dijon mustard, and garlic, it hits all the flavor notes you want in a Caesar salad, but without the lettuce.

SERVES 2 TO 4

1. In a liquid measuring cup, whisk together the olive oil, vinegar, Worcestershire, parmesan, mustard, garlic, anchovies, and salt and pepper to taste. Place the cauliflower head upside down on a cutting board and use a paring knife to make an "x" through the full length of the core. Transfer the cauliflower head to a large bowl and pour half the dressing over it. Turn the cauliflower head to coat it in the dressing, then let it rest, stem-side up, in the dressing for at least 10 minutes and up to 30 minutes to allow the dressing to seep into all its nooks and crannies.

2. Transfer the cauliflower head, stem-side down, to the air fryer and cook at 340°F for 25 minutes. Drizzle the remaining dressing over the cauliflower and cook at 400°F until the top of the cauliflower is golden brown and the core is tender, about 5 minutes more.

3. Remove the basket from the air fryer and transfer the cauliflower to a large plate. Sprinkle with the parsley, if you like, and serve hot.

CARAMELIZED EGGPLANT WITH HARISSA YOGURT

1 medium **eggplant** (about ¾ pound), cut crosswise into ½-inch-thick slices and quartered

2 tablespoons **vegetable oil**

Kosher salt and **freshly ground black pepper**

½ cup **plain yogurt** (not Greek)

2 tablespoons **harissa paste** (see Note)

1 **garlic clove**, grated on a Microplane grater

2 teaspoons **honey**

Note:

Harissa is a spicy, slightly smoky condiment that hails from North Africa. If you can't find it, simply substitute 2 tablespoons tomato paste mixed with 1 tablespoon chili powder and ¼ teaspoon cayenne pepper.

Years ago while working in the test kitchen of *Saveur* magazine, I fell in love with a technique for cooking eggplant that involved deep-frying small pieces until caramelized and tender. The process produced an ethereally smooth, custard-like texture in the eggplant, but also made it pretty greasy, something I just dealt with by dabbing at it with what seemed like an entire roll of paper towels. I was so happy when I tried that same technique in the air fryer, and this has become one of my favorite recipes in the book. Not only do I get an equally wonderful texture, but I have a healthier version without anywhere near the mess to clean up anymore. Try it, and I think you'll be a convert, too.

SERVES 2

1. In a bowl, toss together the eggplant and oil, season with salt and pepper, and toss to coat evenly. Transfer to the air fryer and cook at 400°F, shaking the basket every 5 minutes, until the eggplant is caramelized and tender, about 15 minutes.

2. Meanwhile, in a small bowl, whisk together the yogurt, harissa, and garlic, then spread onto a serving plate.

3. Pile the warm eggplant over the yogurt and drizzle with the honey just before serving.

CHARRED SWEET POTATOES
WITH SMOKED SALT AND HONEY

Sweet potatoes might be my favorite vegetable ever, so I'm always excited to find new ways to cook them. I love lightly charring their skins to offset their sweetness with smokiness and a pleasant bitterness, and the air fryer does the job remarkably well. I use small sweet potatoes so they cook through really quickly by the time the skin is crisp and blistered. A drizzle of honey imbued with smoked paprika rounds out the smoky-sweet dynamic.

SERVES 2

4 small **sweet potatoes**, scrubbed clean (3 ounces each)

2 tablespoons **olive oil**

Kosher salt and **freshly ground black pepper**

2 tablespoons **honey**

½ teaspoon **smoked paprika**

Smoked or **regular sea salt**, for serving

1. In a bowl, toss together the sweet potatoes and olive oil, season with kosher salt and pepper, and toss again to coat evenly. Transfer the sweet potatoes to the air fryer and cook at 375°F, flipping halfway through, until tender on the inside and the skins are crisp and slightly blistered, about 20 minutes.

2. Meanwhile, in a small bowl, mix together the honey and smoked paprika.

3. When the potatoes are done, split them down the middle like a baked potato and lightly press the ends toward the middle to expose the flesh. Transfer to plates, drizzle with the paprika honey, and sprinkle with the smoked salt before serving.

TINGLY CHILI-ROASTED BROCCOLI

With all the spices and products available on Amazon now, it's amazing to see cooks all over the country embracing ingredients that were once rarities in American cookery. One of those is Sichuan peppercorns with their floral, tingly heat that is addictive to experience. I love seasoning broccoli, or any member of the cabbage family, with them to add interest to an otherwise bland vegetable. Here broccoli gets sauced in the fragrant pepper, along with hot chili oil and fresh ginger for even more zip, then air fried until crispy and tender.

SERVES 2

12 ounces **broccoli florets**

2 tablespoons **Asian hot chili oil**

1 teaspoon ground **Sichuan peppercorns** (or black pepper)

2 **garlic cloves**, finely chopped

One 2-inch piece fresh **ginger**, peeled and finely chopped

Kosher salt and **freshly ground black pepper**

1. In a bowl, toss together the broccoli, chili oil, Sichuan peppercorns, garlic, ginger, and salt and black pepper to taste.

2. Transfer to the air fryer and cook at 375°F, shaking the basket halfway through, until lightly charred and tender, about 10 minutes. Remove the pan from the air fryer and serve warm.

SWEET-AND-SOUR
BRUSSELS SPROUTS

¼ cup **Thai sweet chili sauce**

2 tablespoons **black vinegar** or **balsamic vinegar**

½ teaspoon **hot sauce**, such as Tabasco

8 ounces **Brussels sprouts**, trimmed (large sprouts halved)

2 small **shallots**, cut into ¼-inch-thick slices

Kosher salt and **freshly ground black pepper**

2 teaspoons lightly packed fresh **cilantro leaves**

I don't think many people these days need to be convinced that roasted Brussels sprouts are amazing. That said, glazed Brussels sprouts are even better. Cooked until tender and caramelized, then glazed in a spicy-sweet sauce, these Brussels sprouts are incredibly addictive to eat. Despite being glazed in sauce, the Brussels still get crispy and lightly charred, and the sauce gets reduced until sticky and sweet. These make a great side dish, but also a better-for-you bar or cocktail snack, like they do at Prune restaurant in New York, where they set out a bowlful of plain sprouts with toothpicks for stabbing.

SERVES 2

1. In a large bowl, whisk together the chili sauce, vinegar, and hot sauce. Add the Brussels sprouts and shallots, season with salt and pepper, and toss to combine. Scrape the Brussels sprouts and sauce into a 7-inch round cake pan insert, metal cake pan, or foil pan.

2. Place the pan in the air fryer and cook at 375°F, stirring every 5 minutes, until the Brussels sprouts are tender and the sauce is reduced to a sticky glaze, about 20 minutes.

3. Remove the pan from the air fryer and transfer the Brussels sprouts to plates. Sprinkle with the cilantro and serve warm.

SPICY TAHINI-LEMON KALE

¼ cup **tahini**

¼ cup fresh **lemon juice**

2 tablespoons **olive oil**

1 teaspoon **sesame seeds**

½ teaspoon **garlic powder**

¼ teaspoon **cayenne pepper**

4 cups packed torn **kale leaves** (stems and ribs removed and leaves torn into palm-size pieces; about 4 ounces)

Kosher salt and **freshly ground black pepper**

Creamed spinach is one of my favorite steakhouse sides, but the amount of cream that goes into it often makes me not feel so well afterward. I developed this (unintentionally vegan) recipe to give me that same warm nourishing feeling, but without the dairy bloat. Tahini and lemon create a remarkably smooth texture for kale, which stands up to the bold flavors and high-heat cooking better than spinach. Serve this as a side dish for any roast meat, or to keep it vegan, serve it alongside Whole Maitake Mushrooms with Sesame Salt (opposite).

SERVES 2 TO 4

1. In a large bowl, whisk together the tahini, lemon juice, olive oil, sesame seeds, garlic powder, and cayenne until smooth. Add the kale leaves, season with salt and black pepper, and toss in the dressing until completely coated. Transfer the kale leaves to a 7-inch round cake or pizza pan insert, metal cake pan, or foil pan.

2. Place the pan in the air fryer and cook at 350°F, stirring every 5 minutes, until the kale is wilted and the top is lightly browned, about 15 minutes. Remove the pan from the air fryer and serve warm.

WHOLE MAITAKE MUSHROOMS WITH SESAME SALT

At the restaurant Upland, in Manhattan, they serve a whole roasted mushroom that is transformative. The mushroom cooks up tender on the inside while the outside is super crunchy and crispy. I wanted to re-create the magic of that dish in the air fryer, and it works beautifully. The mushrooms condense in both flavor and physical structure and the seasonings make it incredibly savory—so much so that it could stand in for meat for a vegetarian or vegan. Try it and you might never eat small mushrooms ever again.

SERVES 2

1 tablespoon **soy sauce**

3 teaspoons **vegetable oil**

2 teaspoons **toasted sesame oil**

1 **garlic clove**, minced

7 ounces **maitake (hen of the woods) mushrooms**

½ teaspoon **flaky sea salt**

½ teaspoon **sesame seeds**

½ teaspoon finely chopped fresh **thyme leaves**

1. In a small bowl, combine the soy sauce, 1 teaspoon of the vegetable oil, the sesame oil, and garlic. Place the maitake mushrooms in more or less a single layer in the air fryer, then drizzle with the soy sauce mixture.

2. Cook at 300°F for 10 minutes. Sprinkle with the sea salt, sesame seeds, and thyme, then drizzle with the remaining 2 teaspoons vegetable oil. Cook until the mushrooms are browned and crisp at the edges and tender inside, about 5 minutes more.

3. Remove the mushrooms from the air fryer, transfer to plates, and serve hot.

ELOTE CORN AND CILANTRO SALAD

As many a city dweller or person without a backyard can lament, easy, frequent grilled food is a rare treat in the summer. But, in the air fryer, fresh corn doesn't have to be such a rarity. Brushed with a little butter, it chars lightly and cooks up tender and crisp at the same time. It's perfect eaten right off the cob, but even better in this side dish reminiscent of Mexican street corn, composed of the cob's shorn kernels, copious cilantro leaves, and a spicy mayo.

SERVES 2

1. Brush the corn all over with the butter, then sprinkle with the chili powder and garlic powder, and season with salt and pepper. Place the corn in the air fryer and cook at 400°F, turning over halfway through, until the kernels are lightly charred and tender, about 10 minutes.

2. Transfer the ears to a cutting board, let stand 1 minute, then carefully cut the kernels off the cobs and move them to a bowl. Add the cilantro leaves and toss to combine (the cilantro leaves will wilt slightly).

3. In a small bowl, stir together the sour cream, mayonnaise, and adobo sauce. Divide the corn and cilantro among plates and spoon the adobo dressing over the top. Sprinkle with the queso fresco and serve with lime wedges on the side.

2 ears of **corn**, shucked (halved crosswise if too large to fit in your air fryer)

1 tablespoon **unsalted butter**, at room temperature

1 teaspoon **chili powder**

¼ teaspoon **garlic powder**

Kosher salt and **freshly ground black pepper**

1 cup lightly packed fresh **cilantro leaves**

1 tablespoon **sour cream**

1 tablespoon **mayonnaise**

1 teaspoon **adobo sauce** (from a can of chipotle peppers in adobo sauce)

2 tablespoons crumbled **queso fresco**

Lime wedges, for serving

BLACKENED ZUCCHINI
WITH KIMCHI-HERB SAUCE

2 medium **zucchini**, ends trimmed (about 6 ounces each)

2 tablespoons **olive oil**

½ cup **kimchi**, finely chopped

¼ cup finely chopped fresh **cilantro**

¼ cup finely chopped fresh **flat-leaf parsley**, plus more for garnish

2 tablespoons **rice vinegar**

2 teaspoons **Asian chili-garlic sauce**

1 teaspoon grated fresh **ginger**

Kosher salt and **freshly ground black pepper**

I helped my friend Andy Baraghani, a senior food editor at *Bon Appétit*, prep and cater a fund-raiser one summer, and he had me grill whole zucchini until it was blackened all over, like a roasted chile pepper, *then* break it up into bite-size pieces, *then* season it with salt and pepper. Seasoning the zucchini after cooking really concentrated the smoky char flavor that the grill imparted. I adapted that technique here, using the air fryer's high heat to lightly char the zucchini before tearing them into pieces and serving them atop a quick, tangy herb sauce made with spicy kimchi that highlights the concentrated brightness of this humble squash.

SERVES 2

1. Brush the zucchini with half of the olive oil, place in the air fryer, and cook at 400°F, turning halfway through, until lightly charred on the outside and tender, about 15 minutes.

2. Meanwhile, in a small bowl, combine the remaining 1 tablespoon olive oil, the kimchi, cilantro, parsley, vinegar, chili-garlic sauce, and ginger.

3. Once the zucchini is finished cooking, transfer it to a colander and let it cool for 5 minutes. Using your fingers, pinch and break the zucchini into bite-size pieces, letting them fall back into the colander. Season the zucchini with salt and pepper, toss to combine, then let sit a further 5 minutes to allow some of its liquid to drain. Pile the zucchini atop the kimchi sauce on a plate and sprinkle with more parsley to serve.

CHARRED OKRA
WITH PEANUT-CHILE SAUCE

¾ pound **okra pods**

2 tablespoons **vegetable oil**

Kosher salt and **freshly ground black pepper**

1 large **shallot**, minced

1 **garlic clove**, minced

½ **Scotch bonnet chile**, minced (seeded if you want a milder sauce)

1 tablespoon **tomato paste**

1 cup **vegetable stock** or **water**

2 tablespoons **natural peanut butter**

Juice of ½ **lime**

Deep-fried okra is a childhood favorite, but it was always so greasy. The wonderful taste of okra was masked by a thick cornmeal breading and the oil itself, so I set out to make a more delicious version here. Dressed in just oil, salt, and pepper, okra in the air fryer cooks up extra crispy and flavorful, no breading needed. A simple peanut and chile sauce, inspired by West African stews that utilize okra as both a thickener and a vegetable, perfectly complements its bold, brilliant flavor.

SERVES 2

1. In a bowl, toss the okra with 1 tablespoon of the oil and season with salt and pepper. Transfer the okra to the air fryer and cook at 400°F, shaking the basket halfway through, until the okra is tender and lightly charred at the edges, about 16 minutes.

2. Meanwhile, in a small skillet, heat the remaining 1 tablespoon oil over medium-high heat. Add the shallot, garlic, and chile and cook, stirring, until soft, about 2 minutes. Stir in the tomato paste and cook for 30 seconds, then stir in the vegetable stock and peanut butter. Reduce the heat to maintain a simmer and cook until the sauce is reduced slightly and thickened, 3 to 4 minutes. Remove the sauce from the heat, stir in the lime juice, and season with salt and pepper.

3. Place the peanut sauce on a plate, then pile the okra on top and serve hot.

MAPLE-ROASTED TOMATOES

Years ago, I ate maple-roasted tomatoes based on a recipe from a "sugar shack" family—those who tap and process maple syrup from trees—based outside Montreal. They would drizzle the fresh maple syrup over tomatoes, then roast them for hours and hours over low heat until they were super sticky and dehydrated. I love the recipe as is, but always wanted to see if I could make them faster. Thanks to the air fryer, I finally got my wish. The tomatoes dry out and condense in a similar way as the original method, while the fryer's high heat caramelizes them lightly with the maple syrup. These little gems are great to pop in your mouth like candy throughout the day, or spoon them over a salad with toasted walnuts and goat cheese for an extra-special salad.

SERVES 2

10 ounces **cherry tomatoes**, halved

Kosher salt

2 tablespoons **maple syrup**

1 tablespoon **vegetable oil**

2 sprigs fresh **thyme**, stems removed

1 **garlic clove**, minced

Freshly ground black pepper

1. Place the tomatoes in a colander and sprinkle liberally with salt. Let stand for 10 minutes to drain.

2. Transfer the tomatoes cut-side up to a 7-inch round cake pan insert, metal cake pan, or foil pan, then drizzle with the maple syrup, followed by the oil. Sprinkle with the thyme leaves and garlic and season with pepper. Place the pan in the air fryer and cook at 325°F until the tomatoes are soft, collapsed, and lightly caramelized on top, about 20 minutes.

3. Serve straight from the pan or transfer the tomatoes to a plate and drizzle with the juices from the pan to serve.

SWEET AND SALTY ROAST CARROTS

The sweetness of roast carrots can often be overwhelming for me. But this glaze, teeming with soy sauce and umami spices, balances out their sweetness. I love these carrots as a great side dish to virtually any roast meat or salad, grain bowl topping, or, like the Maple-Roasted Tomatoes (page 119), as a sort of vegetable candy to snack on throughout the night.

SERVES 2

1½ tablespoons **agave syrup** or **honey**

1 tablespoon **soy sauce**

1 tablespoon **vegetable oil**

¼ teaspoon **crushed red chile flakes**

¼ teaspoon ground **coriander**

¼ teaspoon **freshly ground black pepper**

1 pound **carrots**, peeled and cut on an angle into ½-inch-thick slices

1 tablespoon finely chopped fresh **flat-leaf parsley**

1. In a bowl, combine the agave syrup, soy sauce, oil, chile flakes, coriander, black pepper, and carrots and toss to coat evenly. Transfer the carrots and dressing to a 7-inch round cake pan insert, metal cake pan, or foil pan. Place the pan in the air fryer and cook at 375°F, stirring every 5 minutes, until the dressing is reduced to a glaze and the carrots are lightly caramelized and tender, about 20 minutes.

2. Remove the pan from the air fryer, transfer to a bowl, and sprinkle with the parsley before serving.

TOASTY CRISPY-BOTTOM RICE
WITH CURRANTS AND PISTACHIOS

1 tablespoon **olive oil**

¼ teaspoon ground **turmeric**

2 cups **cooked white basmati, jasmine,** or other **long-grain rice**

¼ cup **dried currants**

¼ cup roughly chopped **pistachios**

Kosher salt and **freshly ground black pepper**

1 tablespoon thinly sliced fresh **cilantro**

Switch It Up:

The cooking time for this recipe is specific to white rices. Feel free to use other cooked grains here, like wheatberries, fregola, or brown rice, but know that it may take longer for the grains to get really crispy on the bottom. And while you're experimenting, change up the spices on the bottom to suit your taste, or just crisp up the rice in plain olive oil to make a crispy rice cake to serve under roast chicken, sliced steak, or any other dish that has lots of delicious juices that the rice can soak up.

Three of my good friends are Persian, and I've had each of their versions of traditional *tahdig*, the Persian rice dish where cooked rice is browned on the bottom, low and slow in the oven, then turned out and served with the crispy bits broken up as a treat. They're probably all going to disown me when they see this air-fried version, but I make no claims to its authenticity. Miraculously, the air fryer produces a super-crisp bottom layer of rice that's crunchy and ready in less than half the time of the traditional method. This version, studded with currants and pistachios, is a great side dish on its own, or, topped with a fried egg, an unusually indulgent breakfast for one.

SERVES 2

1. Combine the olive oil and turmeric in the bottom of a 7-inch round cake pan insert, metal cake pan, or foil pan.

2. In a bowl, combine the rice, currants, and pistachios, season with salt and pepper, then spoon the rice over the oil, making sure to not stir the oil up into the rice. Very gently press the rice into an even layer.

3. Place the pan in the air fryer and cook at 300°F until the rice is warmed through and the bottom is toasted and crispy, 20 to 25 minutes.

4. Remove the pan from the air fryer and invert onto a serving plate. Break up the crust on the bottom of the rice, sprinkle with the cilantro, and serve warm.

SAVORY BREADS

HOMEMADE PERSONAL PIZZAS

For an Asiago, spicy salami, and kale pizza:

4 ounces **store-bought pizza dough**

2 teaspoons **olive oil**

¼ cup packed torn **kale leaves**

5 (1½- to 2-inch-diameter) slices **salami**

3 tablespoons grated **Asiago cheese**

2 tablespoons shredded **low-moisture mozzarella cheese**

Kosher salt and **freshly ground black pepper**

For a cumin lamb, green olive, and feta pizza:

4 ounces **store-bought pizza dough**

2 teaspoons **olive oil**

1½ ounces **ground lamb,** crumbled into small bits

¼ teaspoon ground **cumin**

¼ teaspoon **smoked paprika**

6 pitted **green olives,** roughly chopped

1 ounce **feta cheese,** crumbled

Kosher salt and **freshly ground black pepper**

Personal pan pizzas may seem like they're just for kids because of their diminutive "fun" size, but they're also great for weeknight dinners. Thankfully, these air-fried versions are quick and much healthier than calling for takeout. Plus, the air fryer's unique ability to create a high-heat baking environment with super-fast circulating air gives the pizzas a great crisp crust that's more difficult to achieve in a traditional home oven. These four ideas are just a sampling of the combinations you can make. Feel free to swap out proteins, greens, and other leftover cooked vegetables for those in these pizzas to come up with your own mini creations.

EACH MAKES 1 PERSONAL PIZZA

TO MAKE THE ASIAGO, SPICY SALAMI, AND KALE PIZZA:

Roll and stretch the pizza dough into a 6-inch round. Lay the dough round in the air fryer, then brush with 1 teaspoon of the olive oil. Arrange the kale leaves over the dough, followed by the salami slices. Sprinkle with the Asiago and mozzarella. Season with salt and pepper, drizzle with the remaining 1 teaspoon olive oil, and cook at 350°F until the dough is cooked through and the cheese is melted and golden brown, about 8 minutes. Transfer the pizza to a plate and serve hot.

TO MAKE THE CUMIN LAMB, GREEN OLIVE, AND FETA PIZZA: Roll and stretch the pizza dough into a 6-inch round. Lay the dough round in the air fryer, then brush with 1 teaspoon of the olive oil. Arrange the lamb crumbles over the dough and sprinkle with the cumin and paprika, followed

by the olives and feta. Season with salt and pepper, drizzle with the remaining 1 teaspoon olive oil, and cook at 350°F until the dough is cooked through and the meat is browned and crisp on top, about 8 minutes. Transfer the pizza to a plate and serve hot.

TO MAKE THE MUSHROOM, THYME, AND SMOKED MOZZARELLA PIZZA: Roll and stretch the pizza dough into a 6-inch round. Lay the dough round in the air fryer, then brush with 1 teaspoon of the olive oil. Arrange the mushrooms over the dough, followed by the thyme leaves. Sprinkle with the smoked mozzarella and chile flakes. Season with salt and black pepper, drizzle with the remaining 1 teaspoon olive oil, and cook at 350°F until the dough is cooked through and the cheese is melted and golden brown, about 8 minutes. Transfer the pizza to a plate and serve hot.

TO MAKE THE VEGAN CRUSHED TOMATO AND "PARMESAN" PIZZA: Set a Microplane grater over a small bowl and grate the walnuts into the bowl. Stir in the nutritional yeast and garlic powder. Roll and stretch the pizza dough into a 6-inch round. Lay the dough round in the air fryer, then brush with 1 teaspoon of the olive oil. Arrange the crushed tomatoes over the dough and sprinkle with the walnut "parmesan" mixture. Season with salt and pepper, drizzle with the remaining 1 teaspoon olive oil, and cook at 350°F until the dough is cooked through, the tomatoes are dried out, and the "parmesan" is browned, about 8 minutes. Transfer the pizza to a plate, sprinkle with the parsley, and serve hot.

For a mushroom, thyme, and smoked mozzarella pizza:

4 ounces **store-bought pizza dough**

2 teaspoons **olive oil**

½ cup **oyster mushrooms**, torn into small pieces

1 teaspoon fresh **thyme leaves**

¼ cup shredded **smoked mozzarella cheese**

⅛ teaspoon **crushed red chile flakes**

Kosher salt and **freshly ground black pepper**

For a vegan crushed tomato and "parmesan" pizza:

1 tablespoon **walnut halves**

1½ teaspoons **nutritional yeast**

½ teaspoon **garlic powder**

4 ounces **store-bought pizza dough**

2 teaspoons **olive oil**

2 canned **whole peeled tomatoes**, crushed by hand and drained

Kosher salt and **freshly ground black pepper**

1 tablespoon thinly sliced fresh **flat-leaf parsley**

Asiago, spicy salami, and kale pizza

Mushroom, thyme, and smoked mozzarella pizza

Vegan crushed
tomato and
"parmesan" pizza

Cumin lamb, green
olive, and feta pizza

HONEY YEAST ROLLS

¼ cup **whole milk**, heated to 115°F in the microwave

½ teaspoon **active dry yeast**

1 tablespoon **honey**

⅔ cup **all-purpose flour**, plus more for dusting

½ teaspoon **kosher salt**

2 tablespoons **unsalted butter**, at room temperature, plus more for greasing

Flaky sea salt

When you're planning a holiday meal, or even just a nice dinner, the last thing many of us remember is the dinner rolls. This recipe makes just enough for a large dinner party and, thanks to being prepared in the air fryer, won't take up precious oven space. These rolls are deceptively simple to make but deliver big on flavor. Try replacing the honey with maple syrup or even barley malt syrup, if you can find it, to add a different flavor to the sweet, fluffy rolls.

MAKES 8 ROLLS

1. In a large bowl, whisk together the milk, yeast, and honey and let stand until foamy, about 10 minutes.

2. Stir in the flour and salt until just combined. Stir in the butter until completely absorbed. Scrape the dough onto a lightly floured work surface and knead until smooth, about 6 minutes. Transfer the dough to a lightly greased bowl, cover loosely with a sheet of plastic wrap or a kitchen towel, and let sit until nearly doubled in size, about 1 hour.

3. Uncover the dough, lightly press it down to expel the bubbles, then portion it into 8 equal pieces. Prep your work surface by wiping it clean with a damp paper towel (if there is flour on the work surface, it will prevent the dough from sticking lightly to the surface, which helps it form a ball). Roll each piece into a ball by cupping the palm of your hand around the dough against the work surface and moving the heel of your hand in a circular motion while using your thumb to contain the dough and tighten it into a perfectly round ball. Once all the balls are formed, nestle them side by side in the air fryer basket.

4. Cover the rolls loosely with a kitchen towel or a sheet of plastic wrap and let sit until lightly risen and puffed, 20 to 30 minutes. (If you don't want to tie up your air fryer basket while the rolls rise, place them on a round of parchment paper or foil that's cut to fit the bottom of your air fryer [or a 6- to 8-inch perforated "air fryer liner," available on Amazon and also used as "bamboo steamer liners"]. Let rise, then transfer to the air fryer basket, still on the paper or foil, when ready to cook.)

5. Uncover the rolls and gently brush with more butter, being careful not to press the rolls too hard. Cook at 270°F until the rolls are light golden brown and fluffy, about 12 minutes.

6. Remove the rolls from the air fryer and brush liberally with more butter, if you like, and sprinkle each roll with a pinch of sea salt. Serve warm.

CHEESY PULL-APART GARLIC BREAD

Though bagna cauda, the classic Italian warm dip, is traditionally served with vegetables, I often use it as a dip for warm, crusty bread, letting the oil, vinegar, and garlic soak into every nook and cranny. Inspired by that savory sauce, I simply reversed the ratios and drizzled it over a small sourdough loaf for this pull-apart bread, cut with deep grooves to allow the dressing to permeate it fully. Sprinkled with cheese and baked until bubbling, this will be a crowd-pleaser for a small party or the perfect treat for yourself, say, with a bowl of tomato soup or chili, to cozy up with on a cold night.

SERVES 2 TO 4

1 small **sourdough boule**

2 tablespoons **olive oil**

1 tablespoon **sherry vinegar**

2 teaspoons **Worcestershire sauce**

1 teaspoon **minced anchovies** or anchovy paste (optional)

2 **garlic cloves**, minced

Kosher salt and **freshly ground black pepper**

⅔ cup grated **smoked mozzarella cheese**

2 tablespoons grated **pecorino cheese**

1. Place the sourdough boule on a cutting board and, if necessary, trim its edges so it fits snugly within your air fryer's basket. Cut through the top of the bread in a crisscross pattern, spacing the cuts every ½ inch and making sure to not cut all the way through so the bread stays together.

2. In a bowl, whisk together the olive oil, vinegar, Worcestershire, anchovies (if using), and garlic. Season liberally with salt and pepper and whisk again to combine. Working on a cutting board, drizzle the dressing evenly into all the grooves of the bread. Sprinkle the bread evenly with the mozzarella and then the pecorino.

3. Place the bread in the air fryer, tent with a round of foil, and cook at 310°F for 12 minutes. Uncover the bread and cook until the bread is toasted at the edges and the cheese is golden brown, about 8 minutes more. Remove the bread from the air fryer and serve hot.

Switch It Up:

If you're making spaghetti and meatballs for dinner and want a classic garlic bread to go with it, this recipe is the perfect canvas for it! Just omit the sherry vinegar, Worcestershire sauce, and anchovies, and double up on the garlic. Add a tablespoon or two of melted butter to the olive oil-garlic mixture, if you like, then cook the bread as indicated in the directions, swapping out the pecorino for parmesan, or keeping it as is and adding up to 2 tablespoons grated parmesan to the mozzarella-pecorino topping.

ROSEMARY AND DOUBLE-GARLIC KNOTS

¼ cup **milk**, heated to 115°F in the microwave

½ teaspoon **active dry yeast**

1 tablespoon **honey** or **agave syrup**

⅔ cup **all-purpose flour**, plus more for dusting

½ teaspoon **kosher salt**

2 tablespoons **unsalted butter**, at room temperature, plus more for greasing and brushing

2 tablespoons **olive oil**

1 tablespoon finely chopped fresh **rosemary**

1 teaspoon **garlic powder**

2 **garlic cloves**, minced

¼ teaspoon **freshly ground black pepper**

Flaky sea salt

While they may look intimidating, garlic knots couldn't be simpler to put together and are super quick to make in an air fryer. Their small size is a boon here, as they bake up crisp and golden on the outside and, at the same time, the inside stays fluffy and soft. I use both fresh and dried garlic to really amp up the garlic's intensity, while the rosemary adds a nice herbal balance (sage makes a great subsitute for the rosemary, too). And with just enough olive oil to keep the dough and coating from getting too dry, you don't have to feel guilty about indulging in two . . . or three.

MAKES 8 GARLIC KNOTS

1. In a large bowl, whisk together the milk, yeast, and honey and let stand until foamy, about 10 minutes. Stir in the flour and kosher salt until just combined. Stir in the butter until completely absorbed. Scrape the dough onto a lightly floured work surface and knead until smooth, about 6 minutes. Transfer the dough to a bowl lightly greased with more butter, cover loosely with a sheet of plastic wrap or a kitchen towel, and let sit until nearly doubled in size, about 1 hour.

2. Uncover the dough, lightly press it down to expel the bubbles, then portion it into 8 equal pieces. Roll each piece into a 6-inch rope, then tie it into a simple knot, tucking the loose ends into each side of the "hoop" made by the knot. Return the knots to the bowl they proofed in, then add the olive oil, rosemary, garlic powder, fresh garlic, and pepper. Toss the knots until coated in the oil and spices,

then nestle them side by side in the air fryer basket. Cover the knots loosely with plastic wrap and let sit until lightly risen and puffed, 20 to 30 minutes.

3. Uncover the knots and cook at 280°F until the knots are golden brown outside and tender and fluffy inside, about 14 minutes. Remove the garlic knots from the air fryer and brush with a little more butter, if you like, and sprinkle with a pinch of sea salt. Serve warm.

Note:

If you don't want to tie up your air fryer basket while the knots rise, place them on a round of parchment paper or foil that's cut to fit the bottom of your air fryer (or a 6- to 8-inch perforated "air fryer liner," available on Amazon and also used as "bamboo steamer liners"). Let rise, then transfer to the air fryer basket, still on the paper or foil, when ready to cook.

SAMOSA VEGETABLE POT PIE

Traditional pot pies are a time investment to prepare, as they involve cooking many different elements before the final dish can be baked until bubbling. This version, however, is much simpler: Inspired by Indian samosas, this pot pie is stuffed with potatoes and peas, spiced with lots of fragrant spices, covered in puff pastry, and baked until piping hot in the air fryer. It's spicy, warm, and comforting and, best of all, ready in less than an hour.

SERVES 2

1. In a medium saucepan, heat the oil over medium-high heat. Add the mustard seeds and cook until they begin popping, 1 to 1½ minutes. Add the onion and chile and cook, stirring, until soft and caramelized at the edges, about 10 minutes.

2. Add the garam masala, coriander, cumin, turmeric, paprika, and garlic and cook until fragrant, about 1 minute. Stir in the potatoes, peas, and lemon juice, breaking the potatoes up slightly and stirring until everything is coated in the yellow stain of the turmeric. Remove the pan from the heat, season the filling with salt and pepper, and let cool completely. The filling can be made and stored in a bowl in the refrigerator for up to 3 days before you plan to cook the pie.

3. Working on a lightly floured surface, roll 1 pastry sheet into a 10-inch square, then cut out a 10-inch round, discarding the scraps. Mound the cooled potato filling

3 tablespoons **vegetable oil**

1 teaspoon **brown mustard seeds**

1 medium **yellow onion,** roughly chopped

½ to 1 **serrano chile,** seeded and minced

1 teaspoon **garam masala**

1 teaspoon ground **coriander**

½ teaspoon ground **cumin**

½ teaspoon ground **turmeric**

½ teaspoon **sweet paprika**

3 **garlic cloves,** minced

1 pound **russet potatoes,** peeled, boiled, and cut into 1-inch chunks

½ cup thawed **frozen peas**

2 teaspoons fresh **lemon juice**

Kosher salt and **freshly ground black pepper**

All-purpose flour, for rolling/dusting

2 sheets **store-bought puff pastry,** thawed if frozen

(recipe continues)

in the center of the dough round, then press and mold it with your hands into a 7-inch disk. Cut a 7-inch round out of the second pastry sheet (no need to roll) and place it over the filling disk. Brush the edge of the bottom dough round with water just to moisten, then lift it up to meet the top dough round. Pinch and fold the edges together all around the filling to form and enclose the pie.

4. Transfer the pie to the air fryer, and cut a slit in the top of the pie with a paring knife to vent. Cover the top of the pie loosely with a round of foil, and cook at 310°F for 20 minutes. Remove the foil and cook at 330°F until the pastry is golden brown and the filling is piping hot, about 20 minutes more.

CHEDDAR AND CHUTNEY PUFF PIE

Cheddar and chutney is a classic British sandwich pairing, like peanut butter and jelly in America. Ever since I first had it, I've been smitten with the flavors and use it often in lots of savory bakes, like quiche, monkey bread, bread pudding, and this perfect party appetizer. A spin on the classic baked Brie, I stuff a puff pastry round with aged cheddar and fragrant mango chutney. Feel free to experiment with other cheese-and-relish pairings, like Gruyère with fig jam, goat cheese, and peach preserves, or cream cheese and pepper jelly.

SERVES 1 TO 2

1 sheet **store-bought puff pastry**

3 ounces **extra-sharp cheddar cheese**, cut into thin slices

¼ cup **chunky mango chutney**

Kosher salt and **freshly ground black pepper**

Egg wash

Crackers and **crudités**, for serving

1. With a rolling pin, roll the puff pastry sheet into a 14-inch square. Cut out two 7-inch rounds and discard the scraps (or save for another use). Arrange the cheddar in the middle of one round, then top with the chutney and season with salt and pepper. Brush the edge of the round with egg wash and top with the second pastry round. Use a fork to press and crimp the edges together.

2. Transfer the pastry round to the air fryer and cook at 325°F until the pastry is puffed and golden brown and the cheese is melted inside, about 20 minutes.

3. Transfer the puff pie to a cutting board and let cool for 5 minutes. Cut the pie into 4 wedges and serve warm with crackers and crudités.

XL CHIMICHURRI BEEF EMPANADAS

½ pound trimmed **beef sirloin**, cut into ½-inch pieces, at room temperature

1 tablespoon chopped fresh **flat-leaf parsley leaves**

1 tablespoon chopped fresh **cilantro leaves**

1 tablespoon chopped fresh **mint leaves**

1 tablespoon **olive oil**

2 teaspoons **red wine vinegar**

½ teaspoon **kosher salt**

¼ teaspoon ground **cumin**

2 **garlic cloves**, minced

Freshly ground black pepper

12 ounces **store-bought pizza dough**

Because I love take-out empanadas so much, but could stand to give the habit a break from time to time, I came up with these "extra-large" empanadas. They're large enough to sate you on their own, but are healthier and ready in less time than it takes to wait for the take-out bag from the restaurant kitchen. Pieces of beef sirloin, marinated in fresh herbs, bake up tender while the dough is chewy and soft inside and super crisp on the outside. It's your steak, sauce, and dinner roll all wrapped in one delicious package.

SERVES 2

1. In a bowl, toss together the beef, parsley, cilantro, mint, olive oil, vinegar, salt, cumin, garlic, and pepper.

2. Divide the dough in half and flatten each portion into a 10-inch round. Divide the beef mixture between the 2 dough rounds, then fold them in half to create 2 half-moons. Use a fork or your fingers to crimp and twist the edges of the dough in on itself to seal the empanadas completely.

3. Place one empanada in the air fryer basket, cut a hole in the top with a paring knife to vent, and cook at 350°F until the dough is golden brown and the beef is cooked through, about 12 minutes. Transfer the empanada to a plate and let cool for 2 minutes before serving. Repeat for the second empanada.

SWEETS

LEMON–POPPY SEED DRIZZLE CAKE

For the cake:

1½ cups **all-purpose flour**

2 teaspoons **baking powder**

1 teaspoon **kosher salt**

½ cup **granulated sugar**

6 tablespoons (¾ stick) **unsalted butter**, melted

2 large **eggs**

½ cup **whole milk**

1 tablespoon **poppy seeds**

Finely grated **zest of 1 lemon**

For the syrup:

3 tablespoons fresh **lemon juice**

¼ cup **granulated sugar**

For the glaze:

1 cup **powdered sugar**

1 tablespoon plus 1 teaspoon fresh **lemon juice**

This cake is equal parts classic American muffin and classic British sponge, both enticingly simple to prepare. In an air fryer, the task is even easier. The one-bowl, muffin-style lemon batter bakes up domed and tender, then gets soaked in a lemon syrup before a final hit of lemon in the form of a creamy white glaze.

SERVES 8

1. To make the cake: In a bowl, whisk together the flour, baking powder, and salt until evenly combined. In a medium bowl, whisk the granulated sugar, melted butter, and eggs until smooth, then whisk in the milk, poppy seeds, and lemon zest. Pour the liquid ingredients over the dry ingredients and whisk until just combined. Pour the batter into a greased 7-inch round cake pan insert, metal cake pan, or foil pan and smooth the top.

2. Set the pan in the air fryer and cook at 310°F until a toothpick inserted into the center of the cake comes out clean, about 30 to 35 minutes.

3. Meanwhile, make the syrup: In a microwave-safe bowl, heat the lemon juice and granulated sugar in the microwave, stirring until the sugar dissolves.

4. Remove the pan from the air fryer and transfer to a wire rack set over a rimmed baking sheet. Let cool for 5 minutes in the pan, then turn the cake out onto the rack and invert it so it's right-side up. As soon as you unmold it, use a toothpick to stab the top of the warm cake all over, making as many holes as you can. Slowly pour the warm lemon syrup over the top of the cake so that it

absorbs as you pour it on. Let the cake cool completely on
the rack to allow the syrup to hydrate the cake fully.

5. To make the glaze: In a glass bowl, combine the powdered
   sugar and lemon juice and stir into a thick glaze.
   Microwave the glaze until loose and pourable, about 30
   seconds, then stir until completely smooth. Pour the hot
   glaze over the top of the cake, still on the rack, letting
   it drip over the edges. Let the cake stand for at least
   10 minutes to allow the glaze to set. Transfer the cake
   to a plate before serving.

STRAWBERRY SCONE SHORTCAKE

Individual strawberry shortcakes are a twee tradition that I love to indulge in from time to time. I also love a traditional Victoria sponge, the classic British dessert of large cake layers that sandwich strawberries and whipped cream. For this recipe, I melded the ideas together and make a giant scone split and stuffed with the berries and cream. It's crunchy on the outside and tender on the inside, and is great for dessert, teatime, or an extra-indulgent breakfast.

SERVES 4 TO 6

1. In a large bowl, whisk together the flour, granulated sugar, baking powder, and salt. Add the butter and use your fingers to break apart the butter pieces while working them into the flour mixture, until pea-size pieces form. Pour ⅔ cup of the cream over the flour mixture and, using a rubber spatula, mix the ingredients together until just combined.

2. Transfer the dough to a work surface and form into a 7-inch-wide disk. Brush the top with water, then sprinkle with some turbinado sugar. Using a large metal spatula, transfer the dough to the air fryer and cook at 350°F until golden brown and fluffy, about 20 minutes. Let cool in the air fryer basket for 5 minutes, then turn out onto a wire rack, right-side up, to cool completely.

3. Meanwhile, in a bowl, beat the remaining ⅔ cup cream, the powdered sugar, and vanilla until stiff peaks form. Split the scone like a hamburger bun and spread the strawberries over the bottom. Top with the whipped cream and cover with the top of the scone. Dust with powdered sugar and cut into wedges to serve.

1⅓ cups **all-purpose flour**

3 tablespoons **granulated sugar**

1½ teaspoons **baking powder**

1 teaspoon **kosher salt**

8 tablespoons (1 stick) **unsalted butter**, cubed and chilled

1⅓ cups **heavy cream**, chilled

Turbinado sugar, such as Sugar In The Raw, for sprinkling

2 tablespoons **powdered sugar**, plus more for dusting

½ teaspoon **vanilla extract**

1 cup quartered fresh **strawberries**

Note:

If you want a more straight-edged scone, you can press the scone dough into a 7-inch round cake pan insert, metal cake pan, or foil pan and cook as instructed for the same amount of time.

BOURBON AND SPICE MONKEY BREAD

1 can (16.3 ounces) **store-bought refrigerated biscuit dough**

¼ cup packed **light brown sugar**

1 teaspoon ground **cinnamon**

½ teaspoon freshly grated **nutmeg**

½ teaspoon ground **ginger**

½ teaspoon **kosher salt**

¼ teaspoon ground **allspice**

⅛ teaspoon ground **cloves**

4 tablespoons (½ stick) **unsalted butter**, melted

½ cup **powdered sugar**

2 teaspoons **bourbon**

2 tablespoons chopped **candied cherries**

2 tablespoons chopped **pecans**

I love the flavors of fruitcake and will defend the much-maligned baked good from all its detractors. One way to get people to fall in love with its flavors is to present them in a new and irresistible way. Hence, this monkey bread, using good ol' store-bought biscuit dough tossed with brown sugar and lots of holiday spices, then baked until browned and fragrant. The bourbon-spiked glaze really takes the bread over the top, and candied cherries and pecans get sprinkled on top for extra crunch and holiday flair. If you don't love fruitcake after eating this, then you might want to ask your friends if your new verbal tic is "bah humbug."

SERVES 6 TO 8

1. Open the can and separate the biscuits, then cut each into quarters. Toss the biscuit quarters in a large bowl with the brown sugar, cinnamon, nutmeg, ginger, salt, allspice, and cloves until evenly coated. Transfer the dough pieces and any sugar left in the bowl to a 7-inch round cake pan insert, metal cake pan, or foil pan and drizzle evenly with the melted butter. Place the pan in the air fryer and cook at 310°F until the monkey bread is golden brown and cooked through in the middle, about 25 minutes. Transfer the pan to a wire rack and let cool completely. Unmold from the pan.

2. In a small bowl, whisk the powdered sugar and the bourbon into a smooth glaze. Drizzle the glaze over the cooled monkey bread and, while the glaze is still wet, sprinkle with the cherries and pecans to serve.

GOOEY "SPOON" BROWNIES

Feasting on a warm brownie, topped with
a scoop of vanilla ice cream, is one of
life's simple pleasures—the dance of hot
and cold, chocolate and vanilla, is magical.
Oftentimes, though, you have to bake the
brownies, let them cool completely to
set, then warm them back up. With the air
fryer, they're intentionally left soft in
the middle, so you can spoon the brownie
"pudding" straight into a bowl while hot
and molten and get straight to your happy
place. An important tip: If you don't have
an insert with an easy-lift handle, serve the
spoonable brownies directly from their pan in
the basket since trying to lift the pan out
by tilting it while the brownie is still hot
could cause the liquidy center to spill out
all over your air fryer. Trust me on this.

SERVES 4 TO 6

1 cup **granulated sugar**

⅓ cup **Dutch-process cocoa powder**

½ teaspoon **kosher salt**

8 tablespoons (1 stick) **unsalted butter**, melted

1 teaspoon **vanilla extract**

2 large **eggs**, lightly beaten

¼ cup **all-purpose flour**

½ cup roughly chopped **bittersweet chocolate**

Vanilla ice cream and **flaky sea salt** (optional), for serving

1. In a bowl, whisk together the sugar, cocoa powder, and salt. Then add the melted butter, vanilla, and eggs and whisk until smooth. Stir in the flour and chocolate and pour the batter into a 7-inch round cake or pizza pan insert, metal cake pan, or foil pan. Place the pan in the air fryer and cook at 310°F until the brownie "pudding" is set at the edges but still jiggly in the middle (it may form a "skin" in the middle, but it doesn't affect the taste), about 30 minutes.

2. Let the brownie pan cool in the air fryer for 5 minutes, enough time to grab some bowls and allow the ice cream to soften to the perfect scooping consistency. Divide the gooey brownies among serving bowls and top with a scoop of ice cream and, if you like, a decent pinch of flaky sea salt.

CHURRO BEIGNETS

3 tablespoons **unsalted butter**, cut into small cubes

½ teaspoon **kosher salt**

1 teaspoon **vanilla extract**

1 cup plus 2 tablespoons **all-purpose flour**, plus more for dusting

2 large **eggs**

1 cup **granulated sugar**

2 teaspoons ground **cinnamon**

Vegetable oil, for brushing

Churros and beignets are two deep-fried classics, but they're really only great when they're still piping hot from the fryer, which means enjoying them at their best is often a rare occurence. Here, however, not only have I combined both treats into one, but the air fryer keeps them crisp on the outside and fluffy inside without all the extra oil. Keep extras in your freezer and pop a few in the fryer to reheat whenever the craving hits.

MAKES 16 BEIGNETS

1. In a small saucepan, combine the butter, salt, vanilla, and 1 cup water and bring to a boil over high heat. Add the flour and cook, stirring constantly with a wooden spoon, until a smooth dough forms, about 30 seconds. Transfer the dough to a bowl, let cool for 1 minute, then add 1 egg, stirring vigorously until the dough is smooth again. Repeat with the remaining egg.

2. Transfer the dough to a floured work surface and sprinkle the top with more flour. Pat the dough into a 9-inch square about ¼ inch thick. Flip the dough sheet over from time to time and add more flour if it's sticking to the surface (don't worry about adding too much flour since you will brush it off later). Cut the dough square into 16 smaller squares and transfer them to a foil-lined baking sheet. Using a dry pastry brush, dust off as much of the excess flour as you can on both sides. Chill the beignets on the sheet in the freezer until frozen solid, at least 1 hour.

3. Meanwhile, combine the sugar and cinnamon in a large brown paper bag.

4. Using a pastry brush, brush 4 squares all over with enough oil to coat well. Place them in one layer in the air fryer and cook at 400°F until golden brown and puffed, about 13 minutes. As soon as the beignets are done, use tongs to immediately transfer them to the paper bag and shake them in the cinnamon-sugar to coat. Repeat with the remaining dough squares and cinnamon-sugar in three more batches. Serve the beignets hot.

NUTTY PEAR CRUMBLE

2 ripe **d'Anjou pears**
(1 pound), peeled, cored,
and roughly chopped

¼ cup packed **light brown
sugar**

2 tablespoons **cornstarch**

1 teaspoon **kosher salt**

¼ cup **granulated sugar**

3 tablespoons **unsalted
butter**, at room
temperature

⅓ cup **all-purpose flour**

2½ tablespoons **Dutch-
process cocoa powder**

¼ cup chopped **blanched
hazelnuts**

Vanilla ice cream or
whipped cream, for
serving (optional)

Switch It Up:

*When you're really in the
mood for apple pie, swap out
the pears for tart Granny
Smith apples, then, in the
crumble topping, replace
the cocoa powder with
more flour, add ½ teaspoon
ground cinnamon, and
omit the hazelnuts. Bake as
instructed in the directions,
and serve with vanilla ice
cream for a simple apple
crumble in a fraction of the
time it takes to roll out two
crusts and bake a massive
pie in the oven.*

Pears, chocolate, and hazelnuts are a classic combination that I return to again and again each fall or winter. The sweet, delicate pears somehow stand up to the bitter chocolate and buttery hazelnuts, creating a heavenly flavor trio, especially in this easy-to-assemble crumble. Use whatever pears you like, although I particularly like d'Anjou for their acidity in sweet desserts like this one.

SERVES 2 TO 4

1. In a 7-inch round cake or pizza pan insert, metal cake pan, or foil pan, combine the pears, brown sugar, cornstarch, and ½ teaspoon salt and toss until the pears are evenly coated in the sugar.

2. In a bowl, combine the remaining ½ teaspoon salt with the granulated sugar, butter, flour, and cocoa powder and pinch and press the butter into the other ingredients with your fingers until a sandy, shaggy crumble dough forms. Stir in the hazelnuts. Sprinkle the crumble topping evenly over the pears.

3. Place the pan in the air fryer and cook at 320°F until the crumble is crisp and the pears are bubbling in the center, about 30 minutes.

4. Carefully remove the pan from the air fryer and serve the hot crumble in bowls, topped with ice cream or whipped cream, if you like.

ROASTED PINEAPPLE GALETTE

I love simple fruit galettes, but most recipes feature the same few fruits. For this air fryer galette, I looked to my favorite fruit group, tropical fruits, for some inspiration and came up with this pineapple stunner. Soaked in rum and infused with lime zest, the pineapple bakes up soft and lightly caramelized and is served topped with cold coconut ice cream. It's a cinch to assemble, and infinitely customizable: Simply substitute other tropical fruits like mango, guava, or even just-ripe banana slices for the pineapple, and let your galette creativity expand beyond apple.

SERVES 2

¼ medium-size **pineapple**, peeled, cored, and cut crosswise into ¼-inch-thick slices

2 tablespoons **dark rum**

1 teaspoon **vanilla extract**

½ teaspoon **kosher salt**

Finely grated **zest of ½ lime**

1 **store-bought sheet puff pastry**, cut into an 8-inch round

3 tablespoons **granulated sugar**

2 tablespoons **unsalted butter**, cubed and chilled

Coconut ice cream, for serving

1. In a small bowl, combine the pineapple slices, rum, vanilla, salt, and lime zest and let stand for at least 10 minutes to allow the pineapple to soak in the rum.

2. Meanwhile, press the puff pastry round into the bottom and up the sides of a 7-inch round cake or pizza pan insert, metal cake pan, or foil pan and use the tines of a fork to dock the bottom and sides.

3. Arrange the pineapple slices on the bottom of the pastry in more or less a single layer, then sprinkle with the sugar and dot with the butter. Drizzle with the leftover juices from the bowl. Place the pan in the air fryer and cook at 310°F until the pastry is puffed and golden brown and the pineapple is lightly caramelized on top, about 40 minutes.

4. Transfer the pan to a wire rack to cool for 15 minutes. Unmold the galette from the pan and serve warm with coconut ice cream.

SHORTCUT SPICED APPLE BUTTER

Cooking spray

2 cups **store-bought unsweetened applesauce**

⅔ cup packed **light brown sugar**

3 tablespoons fresh **lemon juice**

½ teaspoon **kosher salt**

¼ teaspoon ground **cinnamon**

⅛ teaspoon ground **allspice**

With an overstock of applesauce in my fridge one day (don't ask), it hit me that applesauce was basically one step away from apple butter, that delectable spread I buy in pricey jars and slather on my morning toast or dollop onto my oatmeal daily. I experimented with tossing the applesauce, along with some sugar and spices, in the air fryer to see if it would blow up or reduce down to a perfect apple butter texture. To my relief, the latter happened, and now I can't stop buying applesauce just to make this apple butter, in half the time it would take to make on the stove and without all the nervous stirring and dodging of napalm-like apple splatters. The mixture will look over-caramelized in some spots and a little loose when it first comes out of the air fryer, but once you stir it together and let it cool completely in the fridge, it miraculously sets up into the perfect condiment.

MAKES 1¼ CUPS

1. Spray a 7-inch round cake or pizza pan insert, metal cake pan, or foil pan with cooking spray. Whisk together all the ingredients in a bowl until smooth, then pour into the greased pan. Set the pan in the air fryer and cook at 340°F until the apple mixture is caramelized, reduced to a thick puree, and fragrant, about 1 hour.

2. Remove the pan from the air fryer, stir to combine the caramelized bits at the edge with the rest, then let cool completely to thicken. Scrape the apple butter into a jar and store in the refrigerator for up to 2 weeks.

ACKNOWLEDGMENTS

The road to completing this book is littered with a million beeps and blinking console lights. Learning the Zen art of air frying was a completely fun and frivolous experience that I never thought I would have. I always thought I was anti-gadget-cooking, but I use my tea kettle, blender, waffle iron, toaster, spice grinder, and mini food processor weekly, if not daily. We cook with these types of gadgets all the time, so when a new one comes on the market, I take the excited, hopeful approach instead of going instantly skeptical. I'm glad I kept my mind open for the air fryer. I had absolutely no expectations going into this book project other than to learn how to utilize the air fryer to make the best food it can . . . and I think I accomplished that.

All thanks to my editor at Clarkson Potter, Jennifer Sit, for approaching me with this project in the first place, believing in my abilities, and remaining patient, kind, and flexible with all my missed deadlines and last-minute changes. Also, to the Clarkson Potter team, art director Stephanie Huntwork, designer Ian Dingman, publisher Aaron Wehner, production team Joyce Wong and Heather Williamson, Stephanie Davis in marketing, and Eryn Voigt in publicity: Thank you all for your amazing work on making the book look the best it can.

I'm forever indebted to my Lafayette League: Photographer Denny Culbert for your insane camera skills in turning my food into luscious food porn of the highest degree. Jo Vidrine, thank you for not just masterfully assisting Denny, but making gallons of coffee every day to keep us on our toes, and for being THE source for all the best local food in Lafayette. Thank you to the food stylist extraordinaire and sandwich whisperer Tami Hardeman-Boutte for your exceptionally hard work all week, finding that perfect balance in cooked egg yolks, striking gold with that cake drizzle shot, and getting as excited about this food as I am. And to Kim Phillips for knowing just the right props, plates, and utensils to bring the food alive on-screen. Jeremy Conner, I can't thank you enough for your patience and good-natured outlook all week in prepping the food and making more mysteriously unrisable bread doughs and "thick" powdered sugar glazes than one person ever should. (Sidenote: Jeremy makes his own flaky sea salt from the Gulf of Mexico [!!!], sold under the name Cellar Salt Co., and it's freaking delicious; and he generously let us sprinkle it over all the air-fried food during the photo shoot. I'm eternally grateful to artisans like Jeremy and the products they make, and I think you all should buy his salt.)

Thank you to my recipe testers, Susan Phuong My Vu and Lukas Volger, for your precise notes and valuable insights into making these recipes truly shine.

And last but not least, thanks to my partner, J., for being my taste tester during the whirlwind weeks of recipe development, and for allowing me to keep the air fryers precariously placed throughout the kitchen for you to trip over each morning while making your coffee. <3

INDEX

Note: Page references in *italics* indicate photographs.